Bringing
"The Imitation of Christ"
into the
Twenty-First Century

✦   ✦   ✦

Bringing
"The Imitation of Christ"
into the
Twenty-First Century

◆ ◆ ◆

William A. Meninger, O.C.S.O.

CONTINUUM ◆ NEW YORK

1998
The Continuum Publishing Company
370 Lexington Avenue
New York, NY 10017

Printed in the United States of America

Library of Congress Cataloging-in-Publication Data

Meninger, William.
    Bringing the Imitation of Christ into the twenty-first
century /
    William A. Meninger.
        p.   cm.
        Adaptation of: The imitation of Christ / Thomas, à Kempis.
        ISBN 0-8264-1101-0
        1. Meditations.   I. Imitatio Christi.   II. Title.
    BV4832.2.M387   1998
    242—dc21   98-20734
                                                              CIP

This book is affectionately dedicated to my two abbots,
Dom Thomas Keating, O.C.S.O.,
former abbot of St. Joseph's Abbey, Spencer, Mass.,
and Dom Joseph Boyle, O.C.S.O.,
abbot of St. Benedict's Monastery, Snowmass, Colorado.
They both brought the imitation of Christ
into the twenty-first century.

Contents

BOOK TWO

Which Invites Us to Have a Life!

BOOK THREE

Which Discusses Spiritual Values and the Ways in which God Consoles and Instructs Us

BOOK FOUR
*An Encouragement to Become and to Live
as the Body of Christ*

Preface

Since it was written in the fifteenth century, Thomas à Kempis's *Imitation of Christ* has become one of the most widely read books in world literature. It has been translated into over fifty languages and was, until thirty years ago, read daily in many of the religious communities in the church. Since the renewal of the church in the 1960s, flowing from the Second Vatican Council, its decline has been meteoric. Not surprisingly the spirituality that it represents is felt to be culturally biased and theologically conditioned so that its expressions are no longer compatible with the religious thinking and self-identities of religious and lay people of today.

However, we must beware of throwing out the baby with the bath-water. While it is true that the particular spirit of the *devotio moderna* that the *Imitation* embodies is no longer current, the message at its heart is still valid as a meaningful expression of Christian ideals. Those insights, which once made the *Imitation* popular, are in fact timeless and this book is an attempt to express them in the idiom of the twenty-first century.

This book is neither a translation nor a paraphrase of the *Imitation of Christ*. But it seeks to preserve its message, especially the essential message of singleness of mind in the pursuit of God through the imitation of Christ and purity of heart.

The numbering of the chapters and the division into four books follows the *Imitation* exactly. The contents of the chapters flows from the *Imitation* as a model. However, where I think the spirituality should be changed by modification, addition, omission, or outright opposition (see Book 1, Chapter 8), I freely do so.

The artificial distinction between the world and the religious life, the lack of any significant emphasis on social justice, the rather simplistic approach to obedience, and the negative intellectual bias which have been responsible for the modern rejection of the *Imitation* have been modified or opposed. I hope that the deeper, essential elements of the *Imitation*'s spirituality such as humility, motivation critique, suspicion of secular values, purity of heart, and the directness of one's pursuit of God have been reexpressed in a manner more apt to be understood by the man and woman of the twenty-first century.

It is helpful to know when we read the many repetitions in the *Imitation of Christ* that it actually is four separate treatises. Translations differ in numbering the Books and the Chapters of the *Imitation*. The numbering used here corresponds to Ronald Knox's translation (New York: Sheed & Ward, 1960).

BOOK ONE

✦ ✦ ✦

Some Useful Advice
for Spiritual Living

◆ 1
Which Urges Us to See the
Life of Christ as a Model

Christ is the light of the world and of every man and woman in it. To walk in his light is to cast off the darkness of our false-self systems. Thus it is of supreme importance for us to consider his life; what he said, what he did, and what his coming to us means.

There is so much in his teachings and examples that can support us in the daily trials of our lives. We often go unaware of these answers to our problems because we do not answer his invitation to "come and follow me."

Everything does not happen at once. The first step of a journey is not its completion. We must begin slowly and wherever we find ourselves. As we conform our lives more and more to Christ's, his Spirit will support and enlighten us.

We are, all of us, actually called to be theologians. By that I mean we are called to think about God and God's revelation of self in the life of Christ, and consider how best to apply that revelation in our own lives.

To listen to a wonderful sermon about the Christian life or to hear the words of a truly inspiring gospel reading means nothing unless we give ourselves to the actual experience of what they tell us. Who is better off: a theologian who writes books about the Christian life, or the Christian who actually tries to live out that life? We do need the theologians, but they have little value without application of their teachings in the daily lives of the faithful.

So many of the things that consume our time and energies are ultimately useless. Yet we pursue them. It is but a chasing after wind to pursue honors or material desires, unless we see these things in their true light—the light of Christ.

✦ 2

Which Teaches Us That Humility Is Knowing the Truth about Ourselves

Just as our eyes have a natural attraction to light and our ears to sound, so our minds are drawn toward knowledge. So to seek knowledge is a good thing. In all our seeking however we must seek understanding. This is what teaches us how to use our knowledge and how to live it out according to the highest knowledge, the wisdom that God gives us.

Socrates urged us to know ourselves as the basic step toward knowing the truth. This is what humility is: true self-knowledge. It is the most basic of virtues. Indeed, humility is the foundation upon which all virtues stand. It is not a popular virtue. Our modern culture does not relish seeing itself as it truly is, but rather seeks to hide under materialism, possession of things, activity, and prosperity—all of which stems from and enhances a false-self system, the very opposite of humility.

I once heard a theologian say that humility was simply knowing where you stood and then pretending that you were two or three steps below that. That is not humility; it is deceit! True humility is the greatest wisdom. To know who we are, where we stand, and what our motivations are will be sufficient to show us our weaknesses, and even for us to sympathize with the weaknesses of others.

✦ 3

Which Deals with the Search for Truth

Jesus is the light, the way, and the truth. The ultimate truth that he offers us is himself. The ultimate expression of the truth which is himself is love. God spoke but one word since the beginning and that word expresses all that God is and all that God has created. This same word leaped from the heavenly throne and became one of us.

To search honestly for truth is to search for God. This is why the church told us at the Second Vatican Council that atheists who truly search for the truth are in reality searching for God. We cannot search for God unless we had already found God because God alone can summon us on the road to truth.

Men and women have broken through many frontiers. We have searched the face of the earth, plumbed the depths of the oceans, and broken the barriers of gravity on the way to the stars. The frontier we must still deal with is ourselves. This is a frontier that will never be decisively conquered because it must be done by each individual. Every man or woman born onto this earth is called to conquer the frontier of self. They are called to know their true selves. To achieve this knowledge is humility. It is the foundation of all virtues and the stepping-stone to every form of knowledge. The knowledge that is open to us today is astounding. The possibilities of genetic engineering, the information explosion, and medical advances are all gifts of God and must be seen by the light of Christ and used in the manner that love dictates.

✦ 4

Which Calls Us to Prudence and Wisdom in All Our Activity

We live in a world that is moving forward with dazzling speed. Youngsters born into this kind of world are not aware of this, but as the pace increases and their youth gives way to age they will find themselves, as older people do today, struggling in vain to keep up. A foundation is needed. A place from which we can assimilate and make sense of it all. We have to avoid getting on every bandwagon that comes along.

I do not like the negative use of the term New Age because for many people it means anything that they do not like. However, the eclectic flurry that it sometimes involves is neither wise nor sound. I have seen people rush from crystals to seances to astrology to UFOs to reincarnation without any solid foundation to hold on to. The same is true of some theological ideas presented within the church. Everything must be balanced against the will of God, which is expressed in activity and speculation based on love proceeding from sound judgment.

✦ 5

Which Speaks Briefly of Lectio Divina *or Spiritual Reading*

Love and sound judgment are to be found where our faith has always recognized them; in the scriptures, in the holy literature preserved for us by sacred tradition since the earliest days of the church, and in the acknowledged spiritual masters of today.

God has given us the scriptures for our edification and to build us up in love. That is the spirit in which they should be read. Love truth and pursue it. Too often we have taken the scriptures as a series of isolated dogmatic statements and used them to hit one another over the head. Is this the spirit in which God gives them to us? Read avidly, sincerely, and willingly the writings of our holy men and women.

✦ 6

Which Deals with the Excuses Our Modern Culture Places before Us

The quickest way to discontent and misery is to read advertisements or listen to television commercials. We are bombarded with what we do not have and things we do not need.

From childhood we are inundated with false promises of happiness simply by purchasing this or that. If we can be the first kid on the block to collect whatever the ad is selling, we will be happy, better than others, successful.

The first step in the pursuit of contentment is to simplify our desires and our lifestyle. Our culture is oriented to increasing our appetites, and causing dissatisfaction with what we have. True peace and quietness of heart is the greatest enemy of crass commercialism.

✦ 7
On Useless Ambition and False Goals

Those who know the truth about themselves, who know their drives, weaknesses, and selfish motivations can move forward. They are free because then they have a choice. They can act in accord with these imperfect goals or they can opt for transforming actions. Not to be aware of these realities, the effects of original sin, is to live in an unreal world with false hopes and expectations.

The values which our society presents as worth pursuing cannot be accepted uncritically. Unfortunately they are presented to us in ways that bring about acceptance not only uncritically but even unconsciously, and we are moved into the mainstream of useless pursuits and false values. What does it profit anyone to gain the whole world yet suffer the loss of one's own soul?

✦ 8
On the Blessings of Friendship

We have many acquaintances and far fewer friends. All are blessings. It is from the ranks of acquaintances that we draw our friends. Friendship leads to and expresses the deepest forms of Christian love. It can and should bring out the best of what is in us. It calls for unselfishness, willingness to see and respond to different points of view, and an acknowledgment of our dependence on others. How sad it is to see someone without friends.

✦ 9
Which Looks at the Value of Obedience

We are all of us subject to obedience in hundreds of ways. It is the only way that a society can function. We must pay taxes, obey traffic laws, educate our children, accept the norms of healthy living. The list is endless. The benefits are likewise. Obedience is an absolute necessity. It becomes problematic when our motives for it are inferior. Love is the only real worthwhile motive, love of God and of our neighbor.

We are naturally inclined to be obedient to those people, laws, and social customs that suit our personality, convenience, and cultural bias. However, when our responses to the circumstances of our lives are based on love, they testify to the presence of God among us. By this let all know you are my disciples, that you have love for one another. This is true obedience.

✦ 10
On the Value of Silence

The chatter and clatter of our daily lives is unavoidable and has a real place in our ongoing movement toward the fullness of God's kingdom. But the precious value of silence as a balanced counterpart is also necessary.

Conversation with friends, courtesy with strangers and acquaintances, are laudable. We can learn a lot about ourselves by paying some attention to our conversations. What do we prefer to talk about? What interests us? Where is the focus of our attention: to answer these questions—which will tell us where our hearts really lie—we need a deliberate, planned silence. Some time for a daily reflection or meditative silence is needed lest we continuously be carried away by sounding gongs and tinkling cymbals.

✦ 11
Which Tells How Peace Must Be Pursued and That Spiritual Growth Must Be Cultivated

Peace is not thrown at us. We must seek after it and pursue it. The same is true of a grace-filled spiritual life. Imagine the benefits if only half the time we spend watching television or reading the daily news were spent on scriptural meditation or spiritual reading.

The butterfly-scattering here and there to fill a moment's curiosity or pursue a transitory entertainment is the expression of a shallow mind. Many of us spend the major parts of our free time in such pursuits. The mature man or woman is a person who knows how to be "at home." They are not afraid of being alone with themselves to face the deepest realties of their lives. God will be very real to them and the happiness, grace, and peace that awareness of God's presence brings will make itself felt. To be happy in any real and abiding sense calls for daily self-discipline and reflective selections in regard to our use of time and activities. Begin with the smaller and easier things. Experience its value. Then you will be better prepared for more significant pursuits.

✦ 12

Which Tells Us of the Value of Our Daily Struggles

There is no real strength without exercise. To be of real health-value, aerobics must be practiced at least three or four times a week. This requires a strenuous effort, but its effects are soon felt and even the struggle itself can be enjoyed.

Difficult situations in our personal life, at home, or at work, are a kind of spiritual aerobic. They force us to look at our real values and offer us the strength to deal with them. If we try to be anchored in God, we will be aware of the grace that supports us. We are never alone in our struggles. A father who loves his child will carefully watch over him while he struggles to stand, to walk. He will not remove the child's painful efforts to grow, but his loving support will be there. God would no more abandon us than a mother would abandon the child at her breast. Adversity reminds us of God's presence and concern for us. We will never in this life be without it. Therefore, we will never be without God!

✦ 13

Which Treats of the Value of Temptations

One of the most frequent kinds of adversity we have is temptations.
No one is free from them even though there are outstanding people
whom we know who seem to be almost free from them. Be assured.
They too are afflicted. Even Jesus was tried by the devil.

Temptations come from the world, the flesh, and the devil. If it is
any consolation, it is impossible to be without them for any great
period of time. We must remind ourselves that temptations are not in
themselves an evil. No matter how severe they are or even how degrad-
ing they may seem, temptations are not sins. Proceeding as they do
from our weakened nature, temptations afflict everyone. They are
calls to virtue. Do you want to know which specific virtues you are
called to practice? Look at your temptations, refer to the virtues you
need to overcome them. Your potential virtues are the other side of
the coin of your potential sins.

How could we grow in virtue if we were not tempted? Temptations
humble us; they show us who we really are—or could be. They humble
us but they also purify and teach us. It is important to deal with
temptations by resisting them from the beginning. Otherwise they will
grow stronger and be harder to overcome. They are not to be toyed
with. Some people play with fire and think they can toy with temptations as long as they stop short of sin. This may be possible for a very
brief while but it leads to disaster. Temptations, like any other adversity,
should turn us to God whose help is always available. What good
would we be if we never felt any affliction? Metal is tried in the fire
or it remains dross.

✦ 14

Concerning Rash Judgments

Doesn't it make sense for us to be more concerned with our own
weaknesses and faults than with those of others? Even the things that
most bother us in others should teach us about ourselves because they

are often the things we fear the most in ourselves. A useful prayer when we find ourselves being judgmental is: There but for the grace of God go I. Give a little thought to your past critical judgments. How often have circumstances proved you to be wrong?

✦ 15

Which Teaches of the Value of Love as Our Motivation

If we have not love, we have nothing. No matter what we do, if it is not motivated by love, it is a chasing after wind. How do we know if our works are motivated by love or by selfishness? Desire for our own interest, hope of reward, and self-will are usually intermixed with whatever we do. Seek God rather than yourself. Do everything for God's greater honor and glory. At least seek to desire this as far as you can. Then you will have the beginning of true charity.

✦ 16

Which Speaks of Bearing with Others' Faults

First, we must accept that we cannot even correct all our own faults, much less those of others. Thus we have to commend both ourselves and others to God. This way we actually turn faults into the cause of something good.

We can do much to correct our own faults but we are severely limited as to what we can do for others. So when we have done all that is reasonably possible, we commend them to God who knows how to handle everything. Be at peace with the failings of others. You cannot even make yourself be the kind of person you would like to be, how then can you do it for others? Give to others all the forbearance, all the understanding, and all the leeway that you give yourself. Bear one another's burdens and so you will fulfill the law of Christ.

✦ 17
Life in Community

It is no small matter to live with others in community whether that be in a family or in a religious community. We have to sacrifice personal preferences for the sake of peace and harmony. The most important response to community living is our attitude, our internal response. To be a Christian is to be a community person. Indeed it is to be among others not as one who sits at table but as one who serves. There are many advantages to community living, not the least of which are the opportunities for demonstrating a real and practical love. Love begins at home.

✦ 18
On the Example of Others

I think of how many wonderful examples of humility, love, and genuine piety we have, both from the past and the present. I wonder what my own life is like compared to them. We know of so many saints in past centuries who served the Lord in hunger and thirst, in labor often seeming to be fruitless, in faithful prayer and loving service. We live today in an age that calls forth the witness of martyrs and confessors in the church and alongside of it. There are prophets all around us, risking their health, wealth, reputations, and even their very lives to cry out against our cultural destruction of spiritual values, of environmental hazards and our selfish disregard of human life even from its very origins. There are people today who suffer as Christ did by bravely challenging their country or even the church itself where they are seen to fail in their mission of loving service and in the example of poverty and humility. Most often for such people, it is not a question of one or two courageous acts, or their own special fifteen minutes of fame. It is sometimes to endure a lifetime of persecution, years of imprisonment, unspeakable torture, and even death.

Like the saints of the past, the saints of today renounce wealth, honors, human dignity, and life itself. Think of the martyrs in Algeria, the martyrs and confessors of the Central African countries, in China and Russia. Consider the price paid by those prophets in Europe and the Americas who raise their voices against political corruption, profiteering, warmongering, drugs, disease, and poverty. They are grounded in prayer and real humility. They walk in love and loving service, not seeking what they may profit by their labors but whom they may protect, heal, and support. The suffering Christ today in our world depends upon them. How lukewarm our own efforts may seem in comparison.

✦ 19
On the Need of Effort to Live the Christian Life

If we are not good living Christians we are whited sepulchers. To be lukewarm in our commitment to Christ is worse than being outright evil. Ardent fervor needs daily nourishment. The nourishment of fervor is prayer.

What a tragedy it is that there are so many nominal Christians. It is equally tragic that we see so many nominal priests and religious, holding on to the surface veneer of their calling as a way of life or perhaps we should say as a way of death. I visited recently a parish where there is no religious instruction for the children, no sermons preached on Sundays, and where the faithful are often denied their rights to the sacraments. There is a priest assigned to this parish who is a pastor in name only and who has a bishop who ignores him, and spends his own time and concerns on matters he deems of greater worth than that of the salvation of souls under his care. This is what happens when a serious, regular, and conscientious reaching out to God in prayer is neglected. A point is reached where even guilt is smothered.

There are so many sources of instruction today on different levels and ways of prayer. There are workshops, retreats, conferences, classes, and days of recollection available to anyone who seeks them, religious, priest, or layperson. We need, at different times of our lives and on the occasions of different trials, different kinds of prayer and meditation. But we need above all to be watchful, alert, and always ready to see and respond to the Lord—sometimes in silent prayer, sometimes in joyful exclamations. The seasons of the year such as lent, advent, Easter time, and Christmas flow one after the other through our lives as do the various birthdays of the saints and the mysteries of the Lord. But we need to respond to them as opportunities to renew our good intentions and deepen our Christian commitment. To fall into various levels of spiritual sloth or neglect is almost inevitable. We are all weak human beings. The real sin is not to fall but to *remain* fallen. Watch and pray.

✦ 20
On the Value of Solitude and Silence

We live in the world, all of us, even the most cloistered contemplative or solitary hermit. What does it say to us? Sometimes it sounds like the cacophony and confusion of a car radio picking up four or five stations at once. At other times it can be the crass infringement of commercialism attacking the ears or the eyes. The overdose of local and world news with its focus on tragedies and private or public calamities besieges us continuously from all sides. It is absolutely essential that we have some way to get away from it all to hear ourselves think.

God is everywhere, even in the noise. However we need to hear God in silence at times or in sounds like the wind in the trees, the waves on the sand, or the early morning cessation of noise in the city streets. We cannot despise or reject the daily noises of human commerce, but unless we can get away from them on a regular planned basis, they will be too much for us.

It is too easy to give in to the escapism of noise. The radio dial, the TV remote, the computer networks are but a fingertip away. We have to seek after peace and pursue it even if it means simply taking the phone off the hook and shutting ourselves in the solitude of our room for a quiet meditation or spiritual reading. The world is too much with us when it never leaves us alone.

If we try to fill the God-shaped vacuum in our hearts with creatures, we can never fear the Lord or love the Lord. God is always present to us, we must allow ourselves to be present to God. There are subtle forms of pride and arrogant presumptions too that try to convince us that we can handle by ourselves the turmoil and confusion of today's culture. These things are valuable if we allow them to turn us to God. They are disastrous if we allow them to turn us to our own meager resources.

We can find great delight and constant consolations in being alone with God, in hearing God speak to us through God's word in the scriptures, in the shared thoughts of holy and zealous men and women, and in the reflections of our hearts. Of course, at times, it will be tedious, boring, and difficult. But how often have you channel surfed through hours of tedious TV programs? Have you allowed that to discourage you in your pursuit of idle entertainment? What do you have to show for the days, weeks, and months of your life spent before the TV set? What if you spent but a fraction of that time in the presence of God in silence and solitude?

✦ 21

Which Deals with Heartfelt Sorrow for One's Spiritual Neglect and for Unloving Activity

In spite of the ever-present dangers of low self-esteem in today's society, we still must keep in our hearts and minds a lively awareness of our need for sorrow. We have been unloving to ourselves, to our neighbors, and to God—and we are prone to repeat it. It is necessary therefore to regret our failures in love and service. Sorrow and compunction of heart should have a real place in our expenditure of energies. They must not lead us to a useless moaning over the past, but provide us with a thrust into the future. Sorrow for sin is not a lethargic regret but a determined hope for living a better Christian life.

✦ 22

Which Considers the Reality of Human Misery

We are going to be miserable people so long as we put our hopes for happiness in anything but God. Summer homes, expensive cars, exotic vacations, the adulation of millions, monuments to our memory—all of these will do nothing for us that is either lasting or of any value whatsoever. Do we not see daily in the news the miserable lives of many people who have all these things? Even those who have them and seem happy have their share of tribulations. Are not the happiest people those who have their share of frugal comfort *and* who seek to extend it to others? Or, at the very least, they are those who possess as though not possessing. They see themselves merely as stewards of God's wealth.

If this life is all there is, wretched indeed are we. The attitude today does not even have the simplistic concept: "Eat, drink, and be merry for tomorrow you die." In terms of this life and what it offers us, we are justified in seeking liberty and the pursuit of happiness. Here is where the pursuit of happiness begins. It is nothing more than the pursuit of God. We are fools if we expect to find it in any complete or lasting sense on this earth.

The frailness of our individual humanity is only multiplied when we apply it to the commonality of the human race. We can do little or nothing for ourselves to avoid age, illness, and the transitory nature of our existence. Using the resources of the entire human race, we still can do little or nothing. Store up for yourselves treasures in heaven. Lift up your hearts to God in patience and grace-filled expectations. Eye has not seen nor has ear heard nor has it entered into the heart of man or woman what has been prepared for those who love God.

✦ 23

Meditation on Death

The paths of this life, all of them, lead but to the grave. It is absolutely essential for any rational human being to keep this always in mind.

This is not a meditation on the futility of our lives and the fleeting nature of human happiness—just the opposite. It is the only way really to make our lives of value and to ensure happiness. Our death is not an end to life but a change in it. What that change will be depends on the direction we give it.

Jesus is the resurrection and the life, and those who believe in him already have eternal life. If we act now while we have the light, we will have nothing to fear when the darkness threatens us. It is while we have life, where we can make free choices, when we have something to give that we make our decisions—life-giving or death-bearing. God places before us good and evil, life and death, and urges us to choose life. The choice of heaven or hell is one we freely make. What did you do yesterday or today? Did you opt for self for all eternity? That is hell, indeed. Or did you opt for God? You still have a choice—but for how long?

✦ 24

A Hard Look at Judgment and the Fruits of Sin

They are fools who live as though there were no death. It reminds me of the man who fell off a fifty-story skyscraper. As he hurtled past the twentieth floor, he said to himself, "It's all right so far!" The idea of a judgment and rendering an account for our lives is not popular today. It is nonetheless inevitable. I think it may be too simplistic to say that God will render judgment. It is our own lives that will do so.

Of what value really are our attachments to creature comforts and the unloving activities they often demand from us.? Even our limited experience shows that happiness in this life is far more likely to result from temperance, forgiveness, prayerfulness, and the following of Christ. We may not always be successful in our efforts but we can start over seven times a day if need be and reach out to claim the victory Christ has won for us.

As far as punishment for sins is concerned, we shall be the determining factor. We make the choices and we reap the fruits. If, however, we take our stand now on the merits of Christ, our poor efforts will be effective. There is vindication for the just and a day of reckoning for the unloving. Your death is real and it is approaching. Do now the things that will comfort you at that moment.

One of the problems that the sophisticated minds of the twenty-first century have with the concepts of heaven and hell is the inadequacy of the metaphors traditionally used to describe them. Hell as a sulfurous cavern of fire and heaven as a blue sky filled with fleecy clouds and cherubs neither frightens nor attracts us. The choice is really one between self and God.

We must, to a certain extent even as the Bible does, use anthropomorphic language and speak of God as judge, or as condemning or rewarding us after death. In fact it is we, our lives, which are the judges. What we choose is not flames or clouds but ourselves or God. Just imagine what it has been like for you when you were cast totally upon your own resources, when there has not been a shred of comfort from any outside source. Can you put up with yourself for all eternity without the possibility of any form of concerned community, shared resources, or the loving compassion of others? This is what we opt for and what we receive when we select self instead of God. We are given freedom to choose. God does not force Godself upon us.

To love God now with all our hearts, minds, and strength is the only way to happiness here and hereafter.

✦ 25

About the Energy We Ought to Give for Worthwhile Living

I am always edified when I see people who are dedicated to jogging or some other healthful form of aerobic exercise. The effort involved is worthwhile because the fruits in physical well-being are soon experienced. However, the health of body resulting from aerobics lasts only as long as we continue the exercises.

We serve God by loving: loving ourselves, others, and God. This is our spiritual aerobics and the fruits of this exercise are equally discernible. God will not be outdone in generosity. We were made to love and everything else was made to make love possible. When we run this course, our efforts are supported by God who offers infinite love as encouragement and as our goal.

A woman once desperately asked God in prayer, after many discouraging trials, "If only you could assure me that I can persevere, l would be satisfied." An answer came from her heart, "Well if I did give you that assurance, how would you act? Just do that and all will be well." Trust in God.

Most often our spiritual development is hindered by one or two weaknesses that seem to be too much for us. We envy people who seem to be free of them. We must remember that no one is free from struggle or trial. Support others in their weaknesses and you will be strengthened yourself. Remember also that temptations are not sins but aerobic exercises toward health. Even when we fall—and the just person falls seven times a day—we simply get up again and begin all over. The only real sin is to remain fallen. If we can look back on a lifetime of getting up over and over, we will be successful Christians.

Have a good and positive attitude. Look about you and see those people, past and present, who offer encouragement by their example. You may not imitate them exactly or be as successful as they are but be uplifted by them and allow your own faith and hope to supply.

Look especially to Jesus. Is there any trial in your life that you cannot find him enduring, especially in his passion and death? Does he not compassionate your own trials of physical suffering, humilities, failures according to worldly standards, abandonment even to the point of despair? Yet he used all of these issues to bring about newness of life for himself and for us. Remember you are called to follow Christ daily. The way of the cross should be seen, however, not to end in death but in eternal life. Keep reminding yourself that anything worthwhile requires an effort. Remember too that God accompanies you, God will make it all worthwhile.

BOOK TWO

◆ ◆ ◆

Which Invites Us
to Have a Life!

✦ 1

About Having a Real Interior Life

"The Father and I will come to you and we will dwell within you."
"Behold, I stand at the door and knock. Those who open will dine
with the savior." Obviously then the kingdom of God is within us.
Does it make sense to seek for it anywhere else?

What does this mean then? Should we all become navel gazers,
focusing our attention and directing our energies within ourselves?
Certainly not. It does mean though that we are God-bearers, we are
presenters of God to one another and even to ourselves. The kingdom
of God will be known by its fruits. Like draws like and the God
presence within us will be drawn to the God presence wherever it
resides, even in the worst of sinners.

Each of us manifests the kingdom in his or her own unique way.
Each one has gifts to offer that are special. Those gifts are shaped by
our individual lives, our particular talents, and our past history even
including our sins. All of these are informed by the ways in which we
receive Christ into our lives and are manifested in accord with our
own Christ personality in whom we live and move and have our being.
The philosophers assure us that action follows being. If our interior
lives are enriched with the presence of God, our activities will be
likewise.

Let's go for it then! Make room for Christ. Push away some of the
interior incidental clutter that takes so much time, effort, and attention.
Everyone of us, no matter how insignificant we are judged to be by
the values of society, have great and important things to do precisely
because we bear within us the kingdom of God.

Don't expect it to be easy. Which of the saints had it easy? Whom
do you admire most as showing forth God's kingdom in the world
today? Does he or she have it easy? Look to Jesus! How easy was it
for him? Jesus has been very up front with us. If we wish to be his
followers, we must take up our crosses daily. Do you think you will meet

with no opposition, no suffering, no misunderstandings, no betrayals? Look to Jesus!

It is most important and helpful for us to remember that Jesus provides us with more than a good example. He does not merely tell us, "You have seen what I did. Go and do likewise." Rather he promises, "Behold, I am with you always." To have an interior life then is more than an inward gazing. It is to live and act with hope and power. It is to live with the expectation that Christ will inform and empower our deeds through the gracious activity of his Holy Spirit.

✦ 2

On Humbleness as a Great Value

I once approached a friend for whom I had great expectations. He had disappointed me by responding to a difficult situation out of his weakness rather than out of the Christ presence I knew was within him. He showed the power of this Christ presence, however, when I reproached him. Instead of defending himself, he disarmed me completely by saying, "I am a weak man and need your forgiveness and prayers." We are humble when we face the truth about ourselves. If we do not face this truth, God has nothing to work with. We cannot make even the first step in that great journey that lies before us.

To be humble, to be willing to accept the truth about ourselves, is actually the strongest kind of protection. Instead of putting up defenses for others to attack, we disarm our attackers and leave nothing for them to fight against. What a conservation of energy both for them and for us! God knows the truth about us anyway, so what's the big deal?

✦ 3

On How Peace Brings about Peace

Happy are the peacemakers. They are truly God's children. The attitudes with which we look out upon the world and upon other people come from within us. We actually create the world around us. An angry man lives in an angry world. An anxious woman lives in an anxious world. A person who has interior, heartfelt peace will radiate peace. Such people will see good everywhere because they are at peace with themselves. They are not suspicious because they themselves are not torn by suspicions.

Peaceable persons will get along even with difficult people. They will know how to give that soft answer that turns away wrath. Everybody gets along with kindhearted, gentle-natured folk. Praise is due to the peacemakers who radiate their own sense of peace even in the presence of difficult folk. Peaceable persons are their own master. Peace is not the absence of enemies but the ability to absorb ill-treatment in a great soul where Christ dwells.

✦ 4

Which Touches upon Singleness of Heart and Purity of Mind

A man or woman with singleness of heart makes a beeline for God without swerving or deviating. When they have purity of mind, they are able to take pleasure in God. Nothing ungodlike occupies their longings or ability to be united with God. We all reflect God's glory, even the unloving. But when our minds are pure and simple, we are more capable than others to reflect God's glory and relish it. To the degree that we desire the dispositions of our hearts to be pure, to that degree we become mirrors reflecting God's love. We also reflect God's wisdom and the range of our vision penetrates to the ends of God's creation. Wherever God is, we see God and we love God. What a wonderful world!

✦ 5

On Becoming a Fair Witness

Haven't you noticed how quickly you tend to criticize others and how sensitive you are to count their offenses while, at the same time, how easily you make excuses for your own faults? What blind guides we are and how loath to cast the beams out of our own eyes. We find it quite intolerable when someone else loses his or her temper, or neglects duties or does not carry their share of the load. To be a fair witness of ourselves, the only way to humility, we have to recognize especially our own faults in the precise areas where we tend to be most critical of others. We must become the objects of our own observation and the subjects of our own criticism. When we are perfect, then we can judge others.

Those faults in our personality that are most persistent are so because there is that in us that does not want to change or even to improve. Certain addictive qualities that we developed early in life, even in childhood, were of some value to us in coping with our environment. We continue to practice these habits without even noticing them. They may have helped us in the beginning, but now they are hindrances. When I was a child I noticed, probably subconsciously, that whenever I responded to my environment (people, places, or things), by doing everything as perfectly as possible—as I saw perfection—I got approval and love. This in itself is all right. But because of the bentness of original sin, I overdid it. I began to demand the same kind of perfection in everything I did and then in everything everyone else did. Seeing the world only in terms of black or white, right or wrong, I began to feel that it was my job to correct every imperfection. I thus became critical and demanding of everyone and everything without even being aware of it. It formed my personality and hindered my feeble attempts to love unconditionally.

This is only one way in which personalities become defective. Virtue stands in the middle and too much or too little of anything (except genuine love) is faulty. Others cultivated defects in their character by thinking or feeling that success is the only way they will receive love and approval. Still others cultivate qualities of uniqueness, separating them from others. Others seek knowledge, or domination, or being useful to others as their claim to approval. And so it goes.

These various additions or compulsions are very subtle. Often significant others notice them in us while we are ignorant of them in ourselves. This is why we must cultivate the habit of becoming a fair witness of our very selves. Some kind of consistent examination of our actions and especially of our motivations is necessary to root them out.

✦ 6

Which Considers the Blessings in Having
Peace of Mind

When you come right down to it, what does it matter what others think of you, good or bad as long as you have a clear conscience. Peace of mind comes from a genuine loving intention in all that you do, strengthened by a sense and presence of God.

There is some value in the praise or criticism of others as long as we are not deceived by it. If criticism affects us adversely, there is probably some truth in it that we are afraid to look at. If we are gluttons for praise, we are probably insecure in our own merits. Can you see then that a certain indifference to the praise or criticism of others is a good thing?

You are what you are and all the praises or abuses of others is not going to make any difference. Others can see and react to your behavior but only you and God know what are your motivations. God knows your heart and only God can be your true judge. Seek the praise that God will offer as God sees your purity of heart, your clear conscience, your loving activity. God will tell you. "This is my beloved child in whom I am well pleased."

✦ 7

On Having a Friend in Jesus

Reach out with joy and confidence to love Jesus and claim him for a friend. We have been given things to use and people to love. Both will disappoint us if they are not seen in the context of our love for Jesus. What an incredible thing it is that God has been self-embodied in our Lord as a knowable, lovable human being. To put our love in anyone less than God can only result in its eventual crumbling like a house built on sand. Only the love of God can promise to be steadfast and lasting.

✦ 8

Which Continues to Rejoice in the Friendship of Jesus

Jesus has but to speak our name in the depths of our hearts to dispel every vestige of loneliness, sorrow, anxiety, or helplessness. Remember when Mary sought him at the empty tomb and grieved because they had taken away her Lord? It only took Jesus to say her name and her sorrow dissipated. He spoke her name because she sought him. What a blessing it is to seek the friendship of the Lord!

What is worth having more than Jesus' companionship? What is more regrettably lost? When we have Jesus we have everything, without him we have nothing. He will not leave us unless we send him away. But why should we ever do that? It would be the act of a fool. Who or what can take his place?

All that we are, everything that is in us, body and soul, reaches out to claim its fullness in Jesus. The Father has created us this way and the Holy Spirit in us cries out for his presence. If we seek to love God at all, it is only because God first loves us. We have indeed something great going for us.

✦ 9

Concerning the Loss of Consolations

Do you remember the story of Job? God was, as it were, boasting about Job's fidelity. Then Satan responded that it was pleasant enough for Job to be faithful to a god who supplied him with health, wealth, reputation, and power. This was, indeed, true, so God removed these things and Job had the opportunity to prove his fidelity. We are all given this opportunity because, at some point, all will be taken from us: friends, property, health, even physical life itself.

We should be grateful to God for everything God gives us, for comforts, material as well as spiritual. Spiritual consolations are especially blessed gifts for as long as we have them, physical discomforts should matter little to us. The experience of those hardened to the ups and downs of the spiritual journey shows that it is not unexpected to be deprived of both kinds of consolations. The Carmelite tradition especially puts great stress on the place of such difficult trials under the names of the dark nights of the senses and of the soul. The withdrawal of spiritual consolations, we are taught, has as its purpose to direct our search toward God for God's sake and not for the sake of God's gifts. The gift of spiritual consolations and its withdrawal have both the same purpose—to strengthen us in singleness of heart and purity of mind.

✦ 10
Which Encourages Us to Be Grateful

One thing we do know is that everything in this life is fleeting. Whether we have spiritual joys, physical discomforts, temptations, material riches, or whatever, it will not last. We do well when for all things we give thanks to God.

When God looked on creation, God saw that it was very good. When God looked on man and woman as God created them, God took pleasure in them because they were made to God's image and likeness. Is all this true now? Is the earth still very good? Are we still imaging the beauty of God? If we are not, whose fault is it? The trials of our lives, even the fruits of our sins, have but one purpose—to lead us back to God. Anything, no matter how pleasant it be spiritually or physically, that does not facilitate our return to God is to be tossed aside. We must try to actually embrace trials, temptations, and hardships even as Jesus embraced the cross. Jesus made our sufferings salvific if we unite them to his.

When we thank God for everything, we acknowledge that God is the source of everything. Therefore we can claim nothing for ourselves. Paradoxically, when we claim nothing, we are given everything, and so again our hearts are filled with gratitude. Be thankful for all things great and small, easy and difficult, joyful and sorrowful. That way everything will serve its true purpose, to lead us to God.

✦ 11
On the Place of Suffering in Our Lives

God is love and offers us much to love. After all we were made to love and there is a certain fittingness, a kind of comfortable rightness to loving. But that is only one side of the coin. When we are overwhelmed by the graces and material gifts of God, it is easy to love and to give God the glory. The proof of love, however, awaits the removal of God's gifts. Only then can we know if we are loving the giver or the gifts.

It is probably impossible in this life to love God perfectly, with no taint of self-love at all. But we are called to try. This is why crosses are valuable. It is hard to say, as some have done, that we should love crosses, but at least we should recognize them as opportunities to show the genuineness of our love, or to use them in our efforts to let our love be genuine. When did Jesus show best his love for his Father? Undoubtedly, when he was on the cross and his Father seemed furthest from him. I doubt that he would have recognized this love at the time. In such situations it is only when we look back that we are able to see them as moments of pure love. After all, if our crosses were felt and recognized as loving moments, they would hardly be crosses at all. They are holy indeed who can relish their sufferings as opportunities to prove their love for God.

✦ 12
On the Way of the Cross

There is really no way out of it. If we are to be followers of Christ, then we must follow him. We must take up our crosses daily. I think though it would be helpful if we could reframe the traditional understanding of the way of the cross. We usually see it as a way of suffering leading to death. Our faith tells us, however, that it is a difficult road with many trials but eventually leading to resurrection.

The trials and sufferings of the way of the cross, intermixed with consolations and blessings, are simply unavoidable. We can repudiate them, oppose them, try to escape them but it will be in vain. How much more sensible to accept them, adapt to them, and make them useful and even salvific. It is even more sensible to love them and be grateful for them because the way of the cross is the road that leads directly to God. There is no other way.

Crosses are everywhere and we cannot escape them. But, after all, our lives need not be only gloom and misery. Jesus has promised that his burden will be light and his yoke easy. But how can this be? Sufferings that are light and easy are not sufferings.

This is an area that I would like to offer you as a challenge. Simply take Jesus at his word. Right now! Accept as completely and unreservedly as you can, with God's grace, whatever crosses are in your lives right this moment. Then count on Jesus to keep his promise. Offer this prayer with me:

Prayer to Jesus

Lord, Jesus, I know that I am called to the way of the cross in my own way just as you were called in yours. Help me to recognize and accept the value of suffering in my life. Give me the grace to know that in this acceptance I am somehow making up for what was lacking in your own salvific suffering for me and for the world. As I accompany you in our ways of the cross, be my support and let me be the support of those around me. I take great confidence in my belief that the way of the cross leads to life. I am grateful for your grace that supports me. I do not understand how, when, to what degree you will choose to be my strength and my joy in this journey, but I believe you will be and I await your promise to somehow make my burden light. Help me to even love this way and be grateful for it as I seek to love you and be grateful for your will in all things. Amen.

BOOK THREE

✦ ✦ ✦

Which Discusses
Spiritual Values and
the Ways in which
God Consoles
and Instructs Us

✦ 1
How Christ Speaks Directly to Us

The Lord is speaking directly to my heart in all the events of my life. Only let me pay attention. Sometimes God cajoles, sometimes God whispers, sometimes God shouts. Often I let other cajolings, whispers, and shouts drown God out. This only happens when I permit it, but I can permit it so habitually that I become unaware of what I am doing. Let me begin now to listen to God's voice.

This is what God is telling me: you are my child and I love you. I want to be your source of contentment, your place of comfort and safety. Stay with me, abide with me, and you will find peace for your soul. I know the power that fleeting attractions have for you and wish you the good use of them. After all, everything that is was made to facilitate love. Only do not turn to them for what they cannot give. Use my gifts unto my service and to show your love for others, but never forget that real happiness lies only in me.

✦ 2
Truth Speaks to Us beyond Mere Words

I speak to God: dear Lord, you have spoken in the past through your prophets and in the fullness of time you have spoken through your son Jesus Christ. Now you speak through the Spirit of your son. While the prophets and the saints have their place, there is but one mediator between you and me, Jesus Christ, speaking in the graciousness of the Holy Spirit. What a privilege, what a joy!

Let me listen to you Lord. Open my heart to hear the words of your power. I know that when your word goes forth from you, it does not return empty. May it bring me with it. I know the value, Lord, of the teachings of your church, of the reflections of your glory in your creation, of the examples and the writings of your saints, but it is precisely because of all of these that I believe that you yourself wish to instruct me personally and immediately. Your holy ones teach me from the outside, they plant the seed. You teach me from within the heart and make the seed grow and bear fruit.

✦ 3

We Should Listen to God's Words with Open Minds and Hearts

God speaks: my child, hear me in the quiet of your heart. Accept my words humbly and affectionately. What I wish to say to you will bring you wisdom, peace, and joy greater than you could receive from all the self-help books, gurus, and philosophers of the ages.

Do you remember how the scriptures record that I used to walk with Adam in the garden in the cool of the evening? Well, I have never ceased my intimate converse with the sons of Adam and the daughters of Eve, with yourself. How regretful that so many of you have stopped listening to me. The world, the flesh, and the devil speak so convincingly to so many.

I have many wonderful things to tell you, and graces to give, which will empower you to great progress. Don't be one of those who refuses to hear. Don't be one of those who will labor day and night for wealth and meaningless material advantage, but who disdains the real treasures I so greatly desire to give you. I can give you real hope if you trust in me. When you hear my advice, you don't have to worry about the interest rates, the cost of living, the relentless competition of others. I make good my word. Yes, I will test your loyalty, but I will also comfort you. Yes, I will rebuke you for your unloving ways but I will also encourage you to grow.

A Prayer

Lord, I admit your goodness and your love. Sometimes I find it hard to speak to you and even harder to listen. You call me to overcome my reluctance, caused certainly by my unloving ways. When I feel least attracted to you, then I need you most. Help me to realize this and to overcome my reticence.

Even when I do not feel it, I know that I was created to love you and be loved by you. I know that I am an object of your concern, your guidance, and your constant attention. There are times when my self-esteem is low and I feel like nothing before you. Other times when things seem to go well, I am so self-efficient that I feel I do not need you at all. Be with me then. Speak to my heart of my dignity as your beloved child and remind me that I cannot catch my next breath without your help. You know me, O Lord. You are my wisdom, my truth, and my way.

You are what you are and all of the praises or abuses of others is not going to make any difference. Others can see and react to my behavior but you know what are my motivations. You know my heart and only you can be my true judge. I seek the praise that you will offer as you see my purity of heart, my clear conscience, my loving activity. You will tell me: "You are my beloved child in whom I am well pleased."

◆ 4

Which Urges Us to Live Simply and Honestly in the Sight of God

God speaks: my child, seek me as your first priority and your other genuine concerns will be taken care of. I am the truth and it is the truth that will set you free.

I speak to God: Lord, it sounds presumptuous of me to say this but I really believe that you want me to walk beside you in true freedom. I also believe that you will be my truth, my teacher, and my guide.

The Lord speaks: my child, if I am to be your truth, then I must remind you of some hard facts. You have been unloving to me, to yourself and to others. I have had to call you to order sometimes in harsh ways. At times I have even had to let you hit bottom in order that you may realize that the only way left was for you to go up. But know that I love you always even if, occasionally, it must be with a hard love.

Remember my child that Jesus came to bring you life in abundance. Life is my great gift to you. Obviously that cannot mean merely life in this world. There is too much here of pain, sadness, confusion, and ignorance. It is a start but only that. The real life you must seek is eternal. Everything must be seen in the light of eternal life. Nothing is of value that will not bring you to that.

Certainly you must enjoy the good things of this life that come from my open hands. However, you must be aware of how quickly they pass away. Do not seek then or put your hopes in fleeting pleasures no matter how legitimate. On the other hand, it is to be expected that you will endeavor to flee from needless pain. At the same time, be aware that all pain or sorrow is not evil. Sometimes it is the only way to eternal life. That is why such things are called crosses. They are painful but necessary. See them also as but fleeting.

✦ 5

On the Beauty, the Power, and the Glory of Supernatural Love

I speak to God: Father in heaven, if I could speak the language of the angels, I could not, even then, begin to praise and thank you for your love. When you give me your love, you give me yourself. Who or what is like you? Let your love be my strength. When I walk in your love, no journey is too far, no burden too heavy. Your love in me draws me to you with a power greater than all earthly drawbacks and worldly attractions. It gives light to my blindness, joy to my steps, confidence to my reaching out, and promise to all of my efforts. Let me love you more than myself and let me love in you all who love you and all whom you love. You who are love, draw me into yourself so that I may love with your love all that you have created and love. Let me dwell in your very heart and let me know that our love reaches out to the entire world, to universes yet unknown to me and even to dimensions of reality unfathomable to my weak understanding. Finally,

Lord, let me be willing to give myself and all that I have for the sake of your love.

✦ 6
Which Is Concerned with the Testing and Strengthening of Love

The Lord speaks: my child, the testing of love is the stuff out of which human lives are made. It is plotted in novels, sung about in operas, praised in poetry, and recorded in history. My real lovers are delighted with me when all goes well and equally delighted when their lives seem to be a shambles. Which is loved, the gifts or the giver? The gifts that you present at my altar represent you. So do my gifts represent me but do not confuse the two. I can remove my gifts and sometimes do. But then I am never more present to you.

Yes, you will be tempted to settle for something less than me, something that has an immediate lure but will not last. Fight it and it will be profitable for you. No matter what the world, the flesh, or the devil present to you, resist them in faith. You may even fall now and then because of your weaknesses, but do not stay fallen. My help, my forgiveness, my grace is always before you. Reach out and grasp it.

✦ 7
On the Fleeting Nature Even of God's Gifts

A friend who speaks with me occasionally on spiritual matters came to express his gratitude to God for a welcome windfall in his business affairs. I was not impressed with this to any great extent, but I did commend him for recognizing God's goodness. Then my friend did impress me when he said, "The last six months have been the hardest, most discouraging, and most depressing of my life. But I also recognized God's goodness during the period and thank God equally for it." That is real spiritual maturity. He had seen that when God withdrew gifts God gave Godself instead. During that six months when my friend was without God's consolations, he knew that he was not without God.

There has to come a time in our lives when we realize that no matter how hard we try, we do not make the ultimate decisions as to what road we tread. At times our comforts will be taken away, our ambitions frustrated, our health threatened. At these times we need friends, advisers, spiritual counselors, whatever, we want to call them. St. Bernard was fond of saying, "Whoever does his own spiritual counseling, has a fool for a counselor." We need someone we can trust who is not personally emerged in our problems.

We need also to be humble. That is, to realize that we are not in total control of ourselves or of anything. It is good practice, when all is going well, when we are basking in the light and comfort of consoling devotions and well-being, to be aware of the other side of the coin. The Lord gives and the Lord takes away. Even Jesus ended his life on a cross. But then resurrection is offered to us all.

✦ 8

On Being Realistic about Oneself

I speak to God: it is wonderful, Lord, that you grace me so that I am able to speak to you person to person. There is nothing that I can tell you, I know. But this is the way that you show me my real self, the truth about myself. You also show me, when I speak to you, your own concern and love.

You show me, Lord, how my unloving ways have been expressions of loving myself too much or too little. I don't have to worry at all about love when I let you show me how much you love me. Even while I am in my sins you love me.

Left to myself, Lord, what am I? I have done nothing to deserve your love. You love me because you have created me. What have I done to merit this? You love me and you have called me to be a member of the body of your Christ. I cannot claim this as a right. Even in this life, you call me to union with you in love. Do I deserve it? The very gift of love, I have turned into selfishness. I have ignored or even repudiated your love by way of pride and even malice. I am amazed at your constancy, your forgiveness, your unconditional love.

When you show me who I am, Lord, I am filled with confusion. But then you show me what you call me to be and who the grace of Christ makes me in the re-creation of your Holy Spirit. I am filled with humbleness and joy.

✦ 9

We Were Made for God and Everything Else Was Made to Help Us toward God

God speaks to me: my child, where are your energies directed? What do you have when your efforts succeed in bringing you prestige or a summer home, or expensive cars, or luxurious vacations? You have just what your labors have sought. How long will these things last? How satisfying will they ultimately be? How sad it is when people seek anything less than me, that is what they will get. You must realize that your hearts were made for me and they cannot rest until they rest in me. If, in your lifetime, you strive to achieve anything less than me, you will get just that. That is what hell is.

All good comes from me and all real happiness. Anything else is deceptive. You can realize this and acknowledge it simply by being grateful and by placing all of your hope in me. Never will you regret it. When my love informs you and all your activities, you will experience real wisdom, true joy, and you will know the power of love.

✦ 10

Which Speaks of the Joy of Serving God

I speak to God: two things, Lord, I must acknowledge: when I was nothing, you brought me into existence as the fruit of your love, and when I sought after something less than you, your love brought me back to you. When I was unloving and unlovable, you loved me. How else could I have moved from sin to grace unless you loved me when I was yet in my sins.

I think myself to be very giving and humble when I admit that everything I have is yours. But it is really mind-boggling when I face the fact that everything that you have, you give to me. Your beloved Son, your Holy Spirit, and your own self are mine. Your grace and your friendship are given to me. All of your creation is placed at my service. What a fool I am to hold back anything of myself from you.

Help me to know the joy of your service. Let me love and serve all whom you love. Let my greatest desire be to advance the fullness of your kingdom, the holiness of your name, and the accomplishment of your will in my loving service.

✦ 11

On Becoming a Fair Witness of Our Motivations

God speaks to me: my child, the bias of self-love blinds you to many things. One simple way to know with some assurance whether you are doing my will or your own, is to see your reaction as to how things work out. If you are doing something for my sake, you will be happy no matter how I make things turn out. If you are upset with results, you can be sure your motives were mixed with self-interest.

No matter what you do, ostensibly for my sake, pray about it first. Do not jump at every good idea. At the same time, do give prayerful consideration to things you find yourself disinclined to do. Sometimes it is wise to follow your own cautions. At other times you will have to be firm with yourself and forge ahead. At all times act prayerfully.

✦ 12

On Learning to Be Patient

I speak to God: Lord, I really need to understand and to practice patience. Peace is often absent and conflicts, sorrow, and misunderstanding are inevitable, no matter how hard I try.

The Lord speaks to me: my child, peace is not the absence of conflict and sufferings, but rather is the ability to deal with those things. Ask those whose lives seem to you to be nothing but a round of pleasures if they are at peace. Nothing short of me will satisfy my children. You may enjoy my creation and the gifts I give you, but beware lest you substitute them for me.

✦ 13
On Obedience

God speaks to me: no one is free from the constraints of obedience. An intelligent and free response to others at work, in the home, in the church will always be called for. We must honor and obey one another for the love of Christ. Beware of making your own will the supreme power in your life. Unless, that is, you never act except out of love. Even then prayer and prudence are needed to make right decisions. Jesus was obedient even unto the death of the cross. Is anything less asked of you?

I would not have you be oversimplistic about obedience, my child. Blind obedience is always questionable. I have given you intelligence, good will, and the need to love and be loved. Obedience is a handmaid not a slave master. Remember again that virtue stands in the middle. Seeing obedience as absolute and rigid can be a means of escaping personal responsibility. It can also be a rod you use to hit others over the head in judgmental reactions.

When you are a superior or a leader in any pursuit, remember always to respect the minds, morals, and maturity of those subject to you. Only too often people in leadership positions use obedience as a kind of traffic control to make life easier for themselves.

When you are subject to authority, remember that reasonable obedience is a virtue and that all legitimate authority comes from me. In the last analysis let love be the motivation for your obedient observances and you will not go astray.

Beware of superficial, external, or grudging obedience. This is not real obedience at all. To be a virtue, obedience must come from a willing heart.

✦ 14

Wherein We Ask, Who Are We That God Is Mindful of Us?

I speak to God: there are times, Lord, when I feel that I am the master of my fate and the captain of my soul. Then there are times when, closer to the truth, I feel like a fool. When I consider your creation, the stars of the heavens, the works of your fingers, who am I? Of what significance am I? When I see the success or the downfall of others, historically and in my own life, who are wiser, holier, stronger than I, I am covered with confusion.

My being, my existence, and my next breath come from you. What room is there for pride in my life? But I will not let this discourage me because your gift to me is to know that with you and me together, nothing is impossible. My strength is in your power, my understanding is in your wisdom, and my hope is in your love.

✦ 15

In Which We Seek What Pleases God

God speaks to me: my child, remember how Jesus prayed in the garden of Gethsemane. His desire was so intense that he sweated blood, yet he said, "Father, not my will but thine be done." Ask me for what you will, but let your bottom line be the same as Jesus'.

Do you remember some things you prayed for in the past, even in your childhood? I am sure you can see now how disastrous some of those requests would be today if I had answered them as you wanted. Do pray for what you feel that you need and even for what you may desire, but always do so with a humble heart. I hold you in the palm of my hand to protect you from harm even from yourself. So always put a footnote to your prayer as Jesus did. Accept my will knowing it is always for your best.

There are four ways in which you receive my love. I want you to know what they are and notice which is the highest. First, I call you by the attractiveness of my love. Second, I allow you to cling to me in love. Third, I let you experience the joys of my love. Finally, and this is the highest expression of love, I call you to union of wills. I grace you so that you desire only what I desire both for the world and for yourself. So trust me and seek the highest love.

✦ 16
Which Tells Where True Consolation Is to Be Sought

I speak to God: I know, God, that I was created for you and that my heart cannot find rest until it rests in you. You have created many good and wonderful things for me to have and to use. Thank you for them. I know, however, that I was created for you and not for your gifts. Let me never be satisfied by them but always strive to reach beyond them to the giver. Every gift, every human comfort, every material advantage is worthless if it does not lead to you. Let me rejoice in the comfort of your presence, which is always with me even when I do not experience it.

✦ 17
In God We Trust

God speaks to me: my child, trust me. Where else would you turn? Certainly not to yourself over me.

I speak to God: Lord, I admit that you care for me more than I do for myself. Help me, then, to realize that whatever you do with me, you are doing for me. Thank you for my joys and sorrows, my peace and turmoil, my rising ups and falling downs. Thank you for the darkness as well as the light, for the crosses as well as the consolations. Forgive my weaknesses, which make me hesitate to realize that everything comes from you and that you love me more than I could possibly love myself.

I know, Lord, that wherever I go, I walk beside you. What road can be too difficult, what journey too long, with you holding my hand?

Be aware of my feebleness, Lord, and even if it is only briefly, show me a glimpse of your presence. When your finger touches my heart, you can transform me in an instant. Give me the patience to await your touch and the faith to know you are with me even when you seem farthest away.

✦ 18
Follow Christ in Bearing Sorrows

Christ speaks to me: my child, try to keep before you my earthly life and my example. I was a man of sorrows and acquainted with grief. See and imitate how gently I responded to ignorance, ingratitude, and rejection.

I speak to Christ: yes, Lord, I have often experienced these same problems in my own life. Sometimes I forget to turn to you and I feel the weight of these things more than is necessary. Thank you for your example and enlightenment. Remind me of the value of my suffering when I join it to yours. Please be real to me when I have to carry my own crosses.

✦ 19
On Reframing Injuries

Jesus speaks to me: my child, are your complaints self-centered? Are others worse off than you? One loving thing you can do is to let your own sufferings teach you compassion for others. This is one of the fruits of my passion—to show that God compassionates the suffering of God's children.

No one but you (and me, of course) can know the extent of your personal sufferings. Try to be patient. I will help you. When you do suffer, no matter what it is, don't dwell on it except to refer it to me. Sometimes you worsen your own wounds by giving them your devoted and exclusive attention. Give me that attention. There is never a victory without a battle or rest without labor. Come to me all you who labor and are heavy burdened, and I will give you rest for your soul.

I speak to Jesus: Lord, I place my weaknesses in your hands. Let me be strong with your strength.

✦ 20

Which Considers Our Weaknesses and Our Sorrows

I speak to God: what really shames me, Lord, are the trivialities of unloving activities that I give in to. At the moment of temptation, they seem overriding but looking back I am ashamed at their pettiness. I am not an evil person, Lord, and I don't give up entirely, but the incessant badgering of temptations wears me down.

It does serve to show me my own weakness and can turn me to you for strength. Let me find my sufficiency in you because then, when I am weak, I will be strong! As a Christian I am called to light, abundant life and peace, but so often all I see is darkness, death, and turmoil. Let me taste of your sweetness in a way that will support and console me even in the face of all my crosses.

I know that when you seemed to Jesus to be farthest away, you were actually closest to him. It was a situation where it was the darkest before the dawn. When he cried out in agony on the cross his sense of abandonment, it was only a few moments before his spirit was commended into your hands.

It is in Jesus that I take comfort. In and through him I realize you commiserate with my human suffering even including my doubts and sense of failure. Let me find my support as he did by going apart frequently to lonely places to be with you. Then when I must be immersed in the distracting activity so much a part of my life, I can be always conscious of your presence, your protection, and your consolations. Then I will know how to find you when I am forced to face the terrors of imposed lonely places.

✦ 21

Which Speaks of the Giver Rather Than the Gifts

I speak to Jesus: Lord, I must tell myself again and again that my heart is made for you and I cannot find rest elsewhere. In spite of myself, I am always looking for contentment in things, in people, in places, in success or honor. Help me to know that I will never be satisfied in anything less than you. When I consider that you have made me for yourself, how can I possibly find any true joy or satisfaction even in your gifts? Knowledge, talent, joy, fame, consolation, even the temporary happiness that I sometimes receive from your bounty is not you. I cannot ever truly rest in any created thing.

Your gifts are wonderful but they are not you, my God. They speak of you but imperfectly. They remind me of you and sometimes even seem to make promises that I know they can never fulfill. Everything I find in them is but a shadow that calls me to seek the light. Only you are truly good, truly beautiful, truly loving.

Let me cry out to you day and night. Let every beat of my heart speak your name and let my every breath call forth my desire to be with you. Everything else is but a chasing after wind.

Lord, let the sorrows and the sufferings I bear in this life serve to remind me of my separation from you. Let me cry out for your embrace instead of hindering my free and swift passage to your presence. Sometimes I do get an inkling that I am the only thing that stands between you and me. But what can I do? You give me this desire for yourself and only you can fulfill it. I will never cease crying out to you and longing for you. Be real to me, Lord. Be my friend.

The Lord speaks to me: my child, your sufferings move me. Your pleas are themselves proof that I am with you even now. If you desire me, it is because I have given you that longing and I will satisfy it. When you reach out to me, it is actually me reaching down to you. I do hear you and the proof of my hearing is the increase of your love for me. Remember that I am love! Just as it is your nature to be incomplete without me, it is my nature to give myself to you. We are one, I in you and you in me. Let your love, set forth by your faith, even now find true completion in your hope.

✦ 22

Which Reminds Us of God's Many Blessings

I speak to God: Lord, if I am to be grateful for your blessings, I have to know what they are. Of course I am aware of some of them, but your wisdom is so great and your bounty so exhaustive that only you can tell me the extent of them. You know the future as well as the past and present of your creation, and of my place in it. I am only aware of some of the things you have done for me but you know them all. I admit my inadequacy both in knowledge and in gratitude.

All that I am or have and, for that matter, all that everyone else has comes from you. Our health as well as our infirmities. our talents as well as our weaknesses, are all in your hands. If I have more than others, I cannot boast of it; if I have less, I cannot complain.

You know, Lord, better than I that I was made for you and you know exactly what I need to come to you. Whatever you give me is sufficient. Help me to realize and accept this. I praise you for what you have given me.

I do have earthly ambitions, Lord. Sometimes I feel that I have not been given as much as others, that my abilities could take me a lot further, as far as earthly values go, than I have been allowed. However, Lord, when I look at the bottom line, I really want to be content with what is, with what you have allowed me to be and to have. I will admit to my insufficiencies and then find my fullness in you.

Every once in a while, Lord, you grace me with a clarity of vision, in which I realize that to accept your will, even as I strive to do whatever I think is right and just, is to be at peace and content. Out of this peace and contentment you allow me not only to let go of the desire for what I cannot or should not have, but to rejoice with and for others who may have those very same things.

✦ 23

Which Considers True Peace and the Freedom That Comes from It

God speaks to me: my child, if you really want it, you can have true peace and freedom.

I speak to God: I do want peace and freedom. Lord, teach me.

God speaks to me: this may be difficult for you to understand because it is so contrary to what you have been taught and what you see about you. There are three things that will give you peace and freedom. Remember too that the opposite of these things brings discord and bondage. Here they are. Be satisfied with less rather than more; do not see yourself as superior to others but be content with a lesser place; at all times, pray with Jesus. "Not my will, O Lord, but yours be done." Work on these three things and experience the peace and freedom they bring.

I speak to the Lord: what you say, Lord, is true. I have seen that when I always seek more, I never have enough. I can be satisfied with less when I put my mind and heart to it. I certainly do live in a society that teaches worldly greed for more and more possessions. Remind me, Lord, when I am giving in to its errors. The times in my life when I have been happiest have been the times when I have not given into selfish ambition or when I have seriously asked myself, "What would Jesus do?"

A Prayer for Light

Lord Jesus, you are the light of this world. Darkness has no power over you. This includes the darkness I experience in my own mind and heart, which blinds me to the way, the life, and the truth you call me to. Calm the storms of temptations that obscure my desires to serve you and my brothers and sisters. Let me experience that inner peace and stillness that you bring even while I seem to be adrift in turmoil.

If I am to do your will, Lord, I need your help. At times I can open my doors to you only the slightest crack. This is enough for you to enter and cause them to be wide open to your love. The things that

I seek apart from you are trash. Let me realize this. Only in you can I find any real satisfaction. My happiness lies in you alone. Lord, come to my help.

✦ 24
Which Considers Our Attitude toward Others

God speaks to me: my child, you have only so much energy, physical, psychological, and spiritual. Expend it wisely. How much time and effort do you give to useless and unprofitable considerations about the lives of other people? I am speaking here about the foibles, scandals, and meaningless disputes of your acquaintances and, perhaps especially, of famous or notorious people. The mass media of today spend enormous newsprint, paper, and television time magnifying stupidities. Rather than waste your time reading and listening to their follies, pray for them. They are my children too. Receive them into your heart in pity and compassion, rather than as objects of curiosity or even disapproval. Above all do not waste your time, energy, and financial resources supporting their inanities. Their wealth and notoriety often depend on your interest in their dissipating activity. Spend your own energy and time in seeking and recognizing my activity in your life. So often I have stood at your door knocking, and you have not heard me because you were busy chasing after wind!

✦ 25
Which Speaks of Growth and Peace of Mind

Jesus speaks to me: my child, always remember that I have left you my peace. It is my bequest to you. Not only have I left you my peace, I even give you guidance, support, and instructions on how to experience it. Remember, I do not give peace as the world gives it.

I speak to Jesus: Lord, teach me!

Jesus speaks to me: strive to become a fair witness of your own actions and their motivations. Try to be aware of how much of your activity stems from addictive or compulsive behavior, and which, therefore, is not really free. Be patient with yourself but also be watchful.

There was once a practice commonly observed in religious communities called the particular examination of conscience. A few minutes was spent each day in going over the events of the past twenty-four hours to observe in what ways our conduct, attitude, and behavior fell short of what they should be. Special attention was given to particular faults that our observation told us had to be worked on. A resolution would then be made to correct them in the next twenty-four hours. This, or some practice like it, is necessary for spiritual growth and transformation. A critical self-observation and spiritual progress go hand in hand.

A spiritually mature person does possess some degree of balance. He or she seeks my will over their own, and thus have a lively hope that sustains them even, or especially, in the face of trials or injustices. Can you praise my name when you are called upon to bear especially heavy crosses? If you can, know that you are traveling on the path of peace.

✦ 26
Which Is Really a Prayer for Freedom

I speak to the Lord: Lord, it is the role of fools to think that they can glide through life without stumbling and without troubles. What I ask of you is not that you make my life trouble-free (because then there would be no growth), but that you give me a mind that is free. Let me love you above all created things. Herein lies freedom.

Lord, the advantages of life in the twenty-first century are many. In no other time in the world's history have so many luxuries and comforts been available even to the poor. Such things as electricity, television, modern medicine, methods of distance traveling, exotic foods, education, were not available in the past even to kings. I have them all and I am grateful for them. I even want to make these things more available to those who have less of them than I do. But, please

Lord, free me from undue attachment to them. Pursuing them can become the primary goal of my life. This is both idolatry and slavery.

Two things I ask, Lord. First that I may use things and love you and my fellow men and women. I am too prone to love things and use people. Deliver me from this, Lord. Second, let me taste of your sweetness! Let me glimpse, however briefly, the joy of your love so that the temptations of the world, the flesh, and the devil may not deceive me. There are many clouds in my life. I need, even if only occasionally, a brief glimpse of the sun.

◆ 27
Which Treats of the Obstacle of Self-Love

God speaks to me: my child, you speak of your fear of attachment to luxuries and comforts, and you do well to wish to be free of them. There is something even more basic that I would warn you of. That is attachment to yourself, self-love. You must strive to love me above all things including even yourself.

You must never despise yourself. You are lovable. You are worthy of love. Yet this love must not be inordinate. Where your heart (love) is, there is your treasure. If you love yourself in the wrong way, you will be dedicated to the pursuit of material gain and empty, transient honors. These will be your treasures because your heart (love) will be set on them. These things will pass away. They are a chasing after wind. If you really love yourself, you will know that I am the only goal worth pursuing. Place your heart (love) in my hands. I will never disappoint you.

Perhaps one service that the mass media do offer you is a glimpse into the lives of people who have power, attention of others, or wealth as their primary goal. Do you realize how often they are involved in lawsuits, alcohol, drug addiction, divorces, and even suicide? Seek after true peace and pursue it.

A Prayer for Wisdom

Lord, of myself I am helpless but I know that you give me your Holy Spirit who makes all things possible. Create in me, then, a right heart. Help me to stop expending my energy on useless worry and unnecessary anxiety. Let me realize that all things under the sun pass away.

I want to be wise, Lord, with your wisdom and to seek first the kingdom of heaven. Then all else will be given to me. Give me the prudence to recognize flattery and the patience to bear with opposition.

✦ 28
A Further Reflection on Peace of Mind

The Lord speaks to me: my child. try not to be unduly affected by the slanders of others. Very often they are made out of thoughtlessness or ignorance without any intent to do harm. Even when they are malicious, try to see what truth may be in them and what value they can have for you. Of course, you must defend yourself from harmful lies but try to do so patiently and without anger. Turn to me for help.

Your peace of mind must not be dependent upon what others, good or bad, say. What do they know of your real motives or, for that matter, your trials and weaknesses? The more indifferent you are to the reactions of others, the greater will be your peace. Do everything for me! I will understand even your failures!

✦ 29
A Prayer When We Are in Distress

Lord, you have the whole world in your hands. You know me and love me, and I will trust in you. When it comes to the bottom line, I do believe that every hardship and temptation that I face is intended by you for my benefit. This is true even when I am personally responsible for my problems. To those who love you all things will work together unto good. Help me to love you and seek first your kingdom. Then everything else will fall into place.

Lord, I will welcome every trial I have to face. I will receive them with an open mind and an open heart, and see them as gifts from you. I will patiently await from each difficult situation an unexpected blessing. And then I will let it go! I will turn my face to you and my open hands knowing from you comes only blessings. Even when I do not, at the moment, experience it, I will trust your promise that your yoke will be sweet and your burden light.

✦ 30
On Seeking God's Help

God speaks to me: my child, come to me when you labor and are heavily burdened. When things do not go well with you, look to me for help, for rest, for peace. At times I allow these trials just so you will turn to me. For many of your problems there is help available to you from many sources. Seek them out and be grateful for them. But in all your seeking, however, seek for me. Sometimes only I will be able to help you. Sometimes only I will be able to understand the depth of your grief, or anxiety, or loneliness. Call on me as Jesus did on the cross—even if it is only to complain. Suffering is often a necessary means to an end and it is my very nature to draw all things to their perfect completion.

Do you think any job is beyond my power or any suffering outside the reach of my love? Try to realize, my child, that this is true not only of your individual sufferings but also of the massive tragedies brought daily to your attention by the communications media. Wars, natural catastrophes, inhumanity: all these are in my hands. I do not claim to be the cause of them; for the most part, they result from the misuse of freedom. Even so I will not let chaos and evil triumph in the world. Neither will I let it triumph in your life. Be courageous, be patient, watch out for me and I will look after you.

The world, the flesh, and the devil are relentless in their attacks. You know this, so why should you be surprised at it? Don't allow these things to discourage you. Let them instead push you into my arms. When you are weak, then you will be strong. The further away from me that you feel yourself to be, the more I am calling you to myself. I am most present to you when you have most need of me.

Do you think that you have reached the end of your goal? Are you presently at the pinnacle of your human and spiritual growth? Are there no transformations left for you to undergo? Then don't expect to be free from trials and suffering. See them for what they are: my ways of calling you to share in the cross of Christ as a means to resurrection.

As well as the gifts of faith and love, I give you the gift of hope. Receive it, grasp for it, demand it especially when you need it most. Let it transform your pains into something positive and allow you to feel, even in the midst of your tears, a deep, sustaining spiritual joy.

My child, we will be realistic, you and I. Sometimes you will be called to cry out with Jesus, "My God, why have you forsaken me?" I will answer you. It may not be immediate or even the way you expect. Do you know how I answered my Son? I permitted him to die and then I raised him to glorious and everlasting life. I will not permit you to seek anything less.

✦ 31
On Looking Inward to See True Values

I speak to God: Lord, my attachment to created things holds me down. I need to be able to discern between legitimate concern for the responsibilities of my state in life, the obligations I have for preserving our earth, the use and development of my talents for the furthering of your kingdom, and the tendency I have to measure worth and success in terms of anything less than you. I'm willing to put all my eggs in one basket as long as that basket is you. I know that anything less can only disappoint me and hinder my freedom.

The contemplative attitude, Lord, is inward. It is not devoted to externals, especially worldly ones such as success, honors, or wealth. I need your help, Lord, because only your grace can raise me up beyond the level of my fallen human nature. Deliver me from my bondage to everything that is not you.

When I take the time to consider it, I am amazed at the time and energy I and others like me give in to passing desires. How much energy I give to the purchase of a new car, the choice of a vacation. Even necessary things like the choice of college for my children or the location of a new house are often so important to me that I devote more energy to them than I do to serving you, Lord, and to looking into my inner self to determine where my true values lie.

The values of my external activities, for good or for bad, are determined by my inner life. When I seek the time for prayer and meditation, and let my activities flow from this source, then I will approach the contemplative attitude. Anything else is a chasing after wind.

Forgive me, Lord, from falling into the modern heresy of judging myself and others by what we do rather than what we are. Often I pay tribute to people when I see them in the process of gaining the whole world and I ignore the possibility of their suffering the loss of their souls. I know that action follows being and that I must be inwardly a true child of God if my deeds are to be worthwhile.

✦ 32
On Letting Go

The Lord speaks to me: my child, it is obvious that to be free you have to be delivered from chains and prison. Do you realize that your chains are of your own devising and your prison is created by yourself? Your freedom lies in letting go of your bonds. Give up your desires for anything less than me and you will be free. Your desires are your bonds and your prisons. They limit your freedom by focusing your energy on possessing transient things that have no power to satisfy you. Even when you possess them, your desire simply increases for further passing fancies. You become hooked every bit as much as a drug addict—never satisfied, always seeking for more. Give up everything you desire for the pearl of great price. Seek the kingdom of God and you will have everything else.

✦ 33
On the Fickleness of Our False Self

God speaks to me: my child, you know how inconsistent and fickle you are. Now you want one thing, then you desire something else.

How much effort does the satisfaction of these whims really deserve? Very often none at all. Look to your real self, the person created in my image and called by my love, and find fulfillment in union with me. You can remain stable and constant only when you fix your gaze firmly on me. Then you will not be shaken by every emotion, desire, and superficial whim that comes your way. Just say to yourself, "Even this will pass away but the love of God endures forever." Let your desire for me be consciously simple, direct, and unwavering.

✦ 34
True Joy Is Found in God Alone

I speak to God: one thing I ask of you, Lord, that I may dwell in your house all the days of my life. When I have you, I have everything. It is true, Lord, that I can find some joy in created things as much as anyone. I love to visit Disney World or Hawaii or Aspen. I enjoy leisurely meals in fine restaurants, symphony orchestras, and trips abroad. But without you, Lord, these things are ashes. Every meal must be flavored with the spice of your wisdom. Every trip must be taken in your company.

When you are my true joy, then I can find joy in all you have created. True wisdom lies in seeing everything through your eyes. Anything else is folly. All the good that I find in created things calls forth your praise and summons my gratitude.

Lord, I deeply regret my blindness. Sometimes I still find myself following blind guides and giving in to the false values of the society in which I live. Sometimes I tell myself that nothing of value comes from my feeble efforts. If I protest and refrain from pornography, others still support it. If I protest my government's aggressive ways toward weaker countries, it seems to do no good. If I protest child abuse and support the rights of the weak or the sick or the elderly, there are still abuses, wars, and starving people.

So I protest, Lord, even when in my heart you speak the answer. I must do what I can and trust in you to produce the fruits. Also, I must never forget that I do these things, however ineffectual they are, for my own sake. What would it make of me if I did not protest? Be my power, Lord. Arise and help me!

◆ 35
Where There Is Life, There Is Struggle

God speaks to me: my child, even though you and your world were created in my image and all that I made is very good, there is much evil present. You live in the midst of it. Its attacks are open and brazen. Certain horrors, such as the deliberate killing of the unborn, are even protected by laws. People in leadership positions who are given the charism of administration abuse it for personal gain. Priests and religious are all too often exposed in scandalous ways. The evil of drugs and the lure of materialism are before you daily.

In the midst of all of this, you must keep your eyes unwaveringly on me. True peace must be sought in me alone. What else have you or earth of heaven but me? Fight bravely and with hope through all these temptations, anxieties, weaknesses, shame, rebuke, and injuries.

Remember the sufferings of my Christ and all the great saints of the past and the present. Like them you must strive for patient endurance and place your trust in me. Yes, I will test you, but only that your strength may grow. Remember when you are weak, then you are strong because you must rely on me. Be strong, take heart, and wait on me.

◆ 36
How to Respond to the False Judgments of Others

God speaks to me: my child, let my strength be yours. Do not be afraid how others may judge you as long as your conscience is clear. What difference does it make what others say when you and I both know that you are walking tall? This is a clear situation in which your attitude can make your burden light. No matter what you do, it is going to upset someone, so don't expect otherwise. When you know what you must do and you feel assured of my grace, act boldly.

You don't have to look very far to see examples of great men and women who gave all that they had in serving the church but who still suffered from the suspicion, scorn, and judgment of others. When we see how often this happened to Jesus, can we expect anything different? Sometimes the best defense is silence. At other times a patient and humble response is called for. Even within the church there are misguided people, even religious, clergy, and bishops whose personal limitations do not permit them to see change as necessary, tension as a sign of life, and asking questions often more important than getting answers. Be patient with them and with yourself. I am served in many different ways.

Do not be afraid of any man or woman when you know you are pleasing me. Keep me always before you and I will support you with my strength. Worry is often a kind of atheism. It means that you have at least forgotten me and my promises. Never underestimate my power and my love that will always uphold you.

✦ 37
How to Give Unconditional Love

God speaks to me: my child, give up the compulsions and addictions of your wounded nature. You will only find me when you put yourself aside. You have at many times and in many ways surrendered yourself to me. Do it again! I will readily repeat to you my promises of love, strength, and joyful expectations.

I speak to God: Lord, how often must I surrender and how do I leave behind me what is after all my own personality?

God speaks to me: this is a pudding that is only proved in the tasting. You must be in a constant state of surrender, always with an open mind and heart. My grace, love, and guidance surrounds you like the very air you breathe. Know that I desire for you everything that is good and that I provide for you all that you need to get it. Do not reject genuine self-growth and honest human satisfaction, but be always mindful that self-help manuals and popular psychology magazines are not divinely inspired. As unpopular as it is in today's world, it is still of unparalleled importance to strip yourself of every vestige of self-will. I call you to unconditional love. Submit to me daily, many times daily, the imperfections of your self-love. As you do this, even though at first it will be only partial, weak, and hesitating, I will perfect it and reinforce it in you. Experience this!

Have you not seen people give themselves to me but without real trust? They place reservations and conditions on their love. You must love and trust unconditionally. Remember how Job cried out. "Even if he slay me, yet I will trust in him." Real freedom is found only in an unencumbered heart. Recall how the seven Trappist monks and several other priests and rligious in Algiers recently showed their trust in their unconditional surrender. It was because they daily offered themselves to me that they were able to make the supreme sacrifice of their lives. I accepted their surrender and took them to myself in a triumph of joy and happiness such that the human heart cannot even imagine. I may not ask you to die for me, but I will ask you to love me every single day. When you allow my grace to flow to and through you unhindered, our union will endure and produce fruits, even in this life, beyond your imagination.

Just as I ask that you give yourself to me fully and frequently, I will even more frequently and more fully repeat my loving promises to give you myself. What is it that you really want? Would you have me give you something less than myself? I am reluctant to do this because I have made you for myself and you will never rest until you rest in me. Anything else that you seek and find will be empty. Die to yourself and be alive to me. Only in this way will you experience the foolishness of your fantasies and the wretched pursuit of anything less than me.

✦ 38
How to Be Free Even When Outwardly Constrained

God speaks to me: my child do not give in to the false external boundaries placed on you by the trials and limitations of the world you live in. True freedom is inward. It is there that you are the master of all that is about you. It is there that you have the upper hand. This is true whether the things, events, or persons who seem to dominate you are purely external or psychological or mental. In the center of your being I dwell with you. Turn to me with confidence even when you are fearful and think yourself to be weak. When you call upon me, I will hear you even in the midst of your fear and feebleness.

Remember how Moses would seek my presence in the tent of meeting whenever he was perplexed, frightened, or incapacitated. He sought me especially when he faced great problems or was beset by danger and threats. This is what you must do. In the very depths of your heart, turn to me in prayer. Take shelter there in the only place where you are truly free. If I do not deliver you from your external bonds, I will show you how to deal with them. I will give you myself and we will deal with them together. When my Son cried out to me in despair from his cross, he seemed to be totally helpless and under the control of others. Yet never, was I closer to him. He was, at that time, but moments away from his resurrection.

✦ 39
In God We Trust

God speaks to me: my child, I know what is truly best for you. Even when you think I am ignoring you, I am arranging things for your best advantage. Are you surprised that sometimes this may mean suffering together with my Son? Never fear! I will lead you through it. You will experience the fruits of trusting in me even here in this life.

I speak to God: Lord, I often experience the inadequacies of my own efforts so I find great relief in setting things in your hands. My concerns, however, for what may befall me, make me slow to trust you and your promises. The world is so much with me.

God replies: anyone who seeks less than me is never satisfied even when he or she seems to be most successful. Look again at the lives of many so-called successful people hyped by your mass media. They often seem to go from success to success as the world judges success. However, even externally judging from their lawsuits, divorces, suicides, and total absence of privacy, there is little real happiness. So don't be anxious about this kind of success that drives people from one unsatisfactory achievement to another. Devote your energies to serving one another and trusting in me for your happiness. I will not let you down.

✦ 40
All That We Have Is Given to Us

I speak to God: Lord, I came into this world naked and I shall leave it with nothing. Everything I have both physically and spiritually has been given to me. You alone are the giver of good gifts. All I have received, even my sufferings, are given by you to draw me to the ultimate gift, the gift of yourself. Oh yes, I am free to accept or reject your gifts. I can develop or bury the talents you give me, but I know that whenever I try to act without a willing acceptance of your grace, I hurl myself along the path to nothingness.

I gratefully admit and accept your understanding and your help. Thank you, Lord, for always being there. I have but to turn to you, to take your loving outstretched hand and I am unconquerable. I have seen little children learning how to walk reject the outstretched hands of their mothers or fathers. They want to be on their own and to some degree, this may even be necessary. Inevitably, however, they soon stumble and fall. Fortunately, their parents' hands are there to catch them and to comfort when needed. Lord, you are to me both mother and father. You permit me the freedom that I need. At the same time you are watchful and caring.

You allow me to seek reasonably the appreciation of others for the work I do for them. At the same time you gift me with humility, which is the ability to face the truth about myself. That truth tells me that, without you, I am nothing. I wish to do everything for you in the last analysis so even when I go unappreciated, it should not really matter. I can even judge my lack of true motivation by the extent to which human failures bother me.

Even knowing all this, Lord, I am flighty, transient, unstable, and subject to all the weaknesses and vagaries of a fallen human nature. I am swayed by the ups and downs of a fickle world. Like all men and women, I must go through the physical, psychological, and spiritual levels of human growth with their joys, sorrows, successes, and failures; yes, even with their sins. You are the one constant I have throughout all this. If I must take pride, I will take pride in you. Not to us, O Lord, not to us but to your name be the glory.

✦ 41

On the Need for Caution

God speaks to me: my child, do not be upset at the honor and praise given to others. Rather rejoice in it. Should you not be pleased when your brothers and sisters are given acknowledgment for their good works? Even when your own efforts and successes are overlooked, turn to me and seek the only kind of comfort and acknowledgment that matters.

I speak to God: Lord, to be perfectly honest, when I pass my life in review, I see that I have been my own greatest enemy. My sins are always before me. I do not speak of sins as a kind of laundry list of transgressions, but as my failures to love: to love you, to love myself, and to love others. These are my failings: to be unloving. I know that when I am able to love truly, then and only then can I do whatever I want. I have nothing to complain about except my own failures. I can never be at peace and content until I am fully united with you. Who else have I in heaven, O Lord, but you?

✦ 42

Peace of Mind Can Come Only from God

God speaks to me: you must not, my child, let your happiness depend on anything less than me. This includes anyone close to you in whatever capacity; spouse, children, or friends. Yes, you should love them but always for love of me. Remember the commandment: love your neighbor as yourself for the love of God. It is for my sake that you must love others if you wish that love to be real, abiding, and everlasting. Anything different from or less than this will only prove to be ephemeral.

As long as you focus your gaze and attention on anything less than me, you will be frustrated and disappointed. Do not let my gifts get in the way of the greatest gift I have to give you: myself! If your total attention is given to created things, no matter how good or noble they may be, then you have no room for the only thing that matters, the one thing necessary—to love the Lord your God with your whole heart and soul and mind and strength.

✦ 43
All Things in Their Places

God speaks to me: my child, knowledge is the principal thing; therefore, get knowledge. But in all your getting, get understanding. This will lead you eventually to wisdom, which will teach you what to do in the pursuit of your knowledge, how to live it out in understanding and where it belongs in the total scheme of things.

Do you understand what I mean when I say that in the twenty-first century knowledge has outstripped both understanding and wisdom? Men and women know now how to destroy the world and are well along in the process of doing it. They advance and use their knowledge without understanding or wisdom. They know how to change rain forests into commercial agriculture, how to build profitable factories while destroying the air they breathe, how to introduce life-destroying agents into their drinking water because of their ignorant haste to produce material goods, how to exploit the poor, and how to deceive one another into believing that the possession of material things is the greatest good.

Pray for wisdom, my child, seek after it and pursue it. Already many of the wonderful gifts I have given you in the ongoing process of my creation have been wantonly lost by the indiscriminate use of technical and scientific knowledge. Did I give you the earth to care for it or to destroy it? Does it make sense, is it wise to pollute your own wells? What kind of a world are you leaving your children? Your commercial and industrial practices not only show a selfish disregard for my gifts, but for one another, and even a suicidal disregard for your very selves and your children.

Pursue wisdom before it is too late entirely. Wisdom is yours for the asking and your seeking it will not be in vain. Know this, however. It can only come from me and it will only be discovered in its practice. You must see things in their proper perspective. What will it profit you if you destroy your whole world and even lose your souls in the process?

I have raised up many prophets in your modern world. They are using every form of media to make their warnings heard. It seems, for the most part, that they are voices crying in the wilderness. Their warnings go unheeded until it is too late. You are foolish children playing with weapons of mass destruction. Already in many areas it is too late to repair or restore the losses. I offer you wisdom to overcome your blindness, understanding to direct your knowledge. When will you heed me?

✦ 44
On Putting First Things First

God speaks to me: my child, if your life is overcluttered with useless pursuits, who is to blame but you? A simple or, at least, a simpler lifestyle is possible for you if you will accept the wisdom I offer. Seek first the kingdom of God and you will have all that you need. If you want to be at peace, be content with a reasonable frugality. Is there really any true value in "keeping up with the Joneses"? Do you have to have the latest in every material gadget? Are you overconcerned with the opinions of others especially when their opinions lack both understanding and wisdom?

I speak to God: Lord, I must confess to my own share in the foolishness of the world today. In my own reckless pursuit of worldly opinion and material gain, I often ignore the wisdom you offer me. I use people and love things, and even risk the loss of my own soul in these follies. I focus all my concerns on things that do not really matter, and ignore the great values you call me to. Sometimes it frightens me when I examine my days and see how much time I devote to vain endeavors, to things that foster my pride, inflate my ego, immerse my life in materiality while I ignore those things that really matter—the things that will bring me closer to your love. Deliver me, Lord, from wallowing in my material interests. Rouse up in my mind and soul a lively desire for the things of heaven.

✦ 45
On Standing Firmly in the Lord

I speak to God: Lord, when I am in trouble you are my sure help. Yes, I can turn to others for help and sometimes I get it. But oftentimes I do not. At times my troubles are of such a nature that only you have the love and the power to come to my aid. Also at times I am so confounded and ashamed that I cannot confide in anyone but you. I know that you will always understand and be compassionate.

St. Bernard tells us that anyone who uses himself for his own spiritual direction has a fool for a director. Lord, let me put my trust in you and realize what a source of strength, grace, and love is put at my disposal. You are a friend who will never abandon me or show inadequacy. I am humbled by your willingness to be my friend.

St. Agatha once said that she had Christ as her foundation and support. And so do I! What does it matter how weak I am or how unfaithful my companions and friends? Why should I be frightened by an uncertain future, the threats of ill-health, or the fickleness of human nature? I will place my trust and my love in your promises. Lord, I will be strong with your strength. My help will be in the name of the Lord who made heaven and earth.

I know from the example of Christ, who was betrayed by his companion who ate bread at his table. Sometimes my friends, possibly without malice, mislead me. They can entrap me in gloating over the misfortunes of others or involve me in idle or even harmful gossip. These can be the same friends who at other times share with me their own faith and love for you, Lord, in marvelous ways. You, O Lord, are my rock and only on you can I stand firm.

Only you, Lord, can see into my heart. You will never lead me astray or betray me. Let me find my interest in you and expend my energies in serving others for your sake.

✦ 46

On Being Indifferent to the Accusations of Others

God speaks to me: my child, what does it matter what others say of you? If their claims are shameful but true, then use them to reform. If they are false accusations, they are but words and a chasing after wind. If what others say really bothers you, it simply shows that you are too attached to passing values. Let me show you what is necessary and deliver you from concern over wrong things.

If you are criticized for your faults, be grateful for the corrections are worthwhile. They will cause you to take a better look at yourself. If the criticisms of others are malicious, they will not harm you if you just ignore them.

Fix your gaze on me. I am the only judge and I know all your secrets. I will judge both the guilty and the innocent. No one else's judgment matters.

What others may say of you, good or bad, is often untrue. At best it is uninformed. My verdict is always true and just. It is also merciful and compassionate. Have recourse to me in all your decisions. Know that I search the innermost depths of your heart and am not deceived by the external appearances of things. The bottom line is my point of view. Nothing else matters. Whatever the truth may be, I am on your side if you want me to be.

✦ 47

Crosses Must Be Carried by Us All

God speaks to me: my child, you have often taken up your cross for my sake. I will not let it crush you, so never lose heart. Keep this promise always before you. The longest life in terms of years is still fleeting—even yours. The time is never far away when every person's toils and troubles will be over. So they really cannot be as important as we would make them.

Continue bravely with your life, your interests, your vocation, and your service of one another. Bear your sorrows and your troubles, even your sins and weaknesses bravely. Let your hope be strong and hold fast to my promise of eternal life. In spite of the ridicule to which it has been put, there is a "pie in the sky." I have created you for happiness and eternal joy with me. Reach out for this blessing and let it be before you in everything that you do, especially in times of suffering. Think about my promises and take joy in them. The time will come when you will see the reasons for all your trials and the fruits of all your endeavors to love.

There are many who have gone before you who have fought the good fight, who have won the race. Let them encourage you and strive to imitate them. You are summoned to companionship with them if only you will persevere through the brief interval you must yet spend on earth.

✦ 48

On the Joys of Heaven and the Sorrows of This Present Life

I speak to God: it is good for me to reflect on the happiness of those who dwell forever in your presence, O Lord. I want to face honestly and adequately the tasks I have here on earth. I want even to seek a reasonable joy and contentment in your service as you call me. Still, I know there is a life that awaits me that eye has not seen, nor has it entered into the hearts of men or women what you have prepared for those who love you. Allow me to yearn for this life to come even as I accept fully the joys and sorrows, labors and rests of my present life.

The crosses of my life are manifold. I live out the bentness of original sin in my own personality and in the wounds of the society in which I must live. I am tormented by cares, worried by my inadequacies, frightened by my weaknesses, and enslaved by my sinful passions. Entangled by foolishness, surrounded by error, and exhausted by temptations, I sometimes find it very hard to see the work of your grace in my life and in the world.

I need to know that these evils will come to an end and that I will be freed from these torments. I yearn for a lasting peace where there will be nothing evil to drag me down in soul or in body. I know that in you, Lord, I will find the full measure of my happiness. Allow me to keep this desire alive and strong so that each day of my earthly life I may reach up to you as my true goal.

Be yourself, Lord, my comfort. Even above your gifts, you offer yourself to me. Sometimes though it seems that when I lift my arms up to you, they remain empty and I become a battlefield where hope and despair, faith and disbelief, love and futility, wage open war. Be not far from me, Lord. Show me your truth and your light. Let your Son, Jesus Christ, be real to me. Let him be my way, my light, and my life. If he is always in my thoughts, then I will always be with him. Even in the midst of the worst struggles of my life, I know that my heart can be with you Lord. You will come to me and abide within me. I beg it of you and open my mind and heart to your presence.

✦ 49

On the Desire for Eternal Life

God speaks to me: my child, the world is too much with you. It is all that you know. All your being, all your faculties are taken up with it. Its legitimate beauties, its inevitable troubles, its lures and preoccupation present themselves as ends in themselves instead of what they really are, a means to something beyond them. The very best of what this world has to offer is not even a shadow of what is to come, which I have prepared for those who love.

I know at times you are able to look beyond the passing blessings and trials of your earthly life to something that far surpasses it. When this happens, it is a pure gift from me. Acknowledge this gift as often as you are aware of it. Thank me for it and recognize my love for you, which is behind it. Your heart was made for me and cannot rest until it rests in me. What a holy longing this is.

At best, however, your desire for a better life, for the blessing of heaven, is mixed with self-love. There is no fire that does not have smoke coming from it. Even when you think that your desire and your prayers are unblemished, there is always an element of self-interest to be found.

Even though this is a holy longing, do not let it make you dissatisfied with your present lot, which is my will for you. I know what you want and what you need. To the extent that your desire to be with me in peace, joy, and love, free from the crosses of earthly life, that desire is given you by your attraction to me. It is because you are in my image that you wish also to be in my likeness free from the wounds and limitations of original sin.

Be satisfied, however, with the war you are still called upon to wage. I am with you in it and it is my way of making you strong and worthy of the great gifts I have in store for you. Nothing in your present life will be wasted if you see my direction in it. Remember that everything, everything, everything leads to God.

Do not be discouraged by your trials. You still have many to undergo. Your prayers will not seem to be answered while those about you are rejoicing in my responses. At times I will comfort you but there will always be something lacking. This is my way of drawing you to full spiritual and human maturity. At these times reach out to the teachings and example of my Son. He has won the victory for you but you still have to claim its fullness for yourself.

Do not be concerned about what others say or do or what happens to them. At times it will seem that I am favoring them, even to your sorrow or harm. If this is what you see, then rejoice for them. Let it call forth from you an unselfish, unconditional love, and you will profit from their good fortune even more than they will.

Hold before you always, my child, the promises I have made to you. I am faithful. Where you are now tied to the bonds and obligations of your earthly labor, you shall be free. Where you are now saddened by the sorrows of your present life, you shall rejoice. Where you are now puzzled and frustrated by your failures and disappointment, you shall receive knowledge, understanding, and wisdom. You are preparing for that time when your will and mine are completely one. My will is that all of your purest desires will be satisfied and that the richness of my glory will replace the drabs of your sufferings. Your weakness will be satisfied by my strength, and your fears by the open and generous sharing of my very life and love.

During your present life then be humble enough to accept the truth as I reveal it to you. Everything leads to me if you will have it so. No pain, no trial, no obstacle will be wasted. Desire only that in all things I may be glorified.

✦ 50
Into Your Hands, O Lord

I speak to God: I bless you, my Lord and father, my God and mother. Only good comes from you and you hold everything in the palms of your hands. I am your child and your servant. Only in you can I find real happiness. All that I have comes from you and all that I can expect will be willingly and lovingly poured out upon me from your hands. If I could only see it, even the aches and pains that so often afflict me are your gifts.

I see others walking steadily in your truth and your light. Once in a while you invite me to join them and I rejoice in your consolations. You flood my heart with joy and I burst out in song with praise. More often than not, however, you call me to walk alone in rough and dark ways. Sorrow and grief fill my heart and I cry out for the peace and joy I once knew.

My Lord, let me be prepared and accept whatever you send me. Let me rejoice equally in suffering and in exultation. As difficult as it is for me to admit, I do think that my heart is enlarged more by sorrow than by rejoicing, and that my weak and immature human nature grows and becomes strong more by carrying crosses than by running swiftly along the road of your consolations. I accept, at least in theory, that there are times when I should expect humiliations, spiritual and physical torments, disappointments, and weaknesses. When you allow these things, accompany them with your loving presence. Reach out and hold my hand. Do not remove them from me as I need them to grow and to prove my love. But do walk with me when I am on that dark and lonely road and it will be enough. Everything, Lord, comes from you and leads to you.

We are told that the Lord afflicts those whom the Lord loves. Jesus tells us to take up our crosses daily and to follow him. I know that you do not permit suffering without an occasional experience of peace and joy, even at the same time as the suffering. But, Lord, I dread the suffering even as I accept it and realize its value. Do not let me waste my crosses, but remind and help me to unite them to the cross of Christ for the redemption of the world. I do admit that one consistent result of all my aches and pains is that they turn me to you even if only to complain. But I know that this too is prayer and an expression of faith.

I am in your hands, Lord, and I accept whatever comes from you. I do not think or feel that my sufferings are deliberately or directly caused by you any more than the sufferings and growth pains of a child are directly willed by its father or mother. But you are a provident, caring, watchful God and all things are in your hands. Help me to accept that pain and disappointment are not necessarily evils, but have a real and useful place in my life as well as in the life of the world. You know what I need, what my weakness can endure, and how to bring good for myself and others from my sufferings united to those of Christ.

My God, grant me knowledge and understanding where I am ignorant. Fill me with your love where I am selfish. Let me rejoice in what is good and turn from whatever is not you. Let me not be deceived by external appearances and by the lures of the world, the flesh, and the devil. Let me pursue directly, relentlessly, and lovingly what I know pleases you. This, I know, will be a win-win situation for your glory and my salvation. Above all, let me always hold before my mind the words of St. Francis: "We are whatever we are in your sight, O Lord, and nothing more."

✦ 51

We Cannot Always Be in the State of a Burning Desire for Holiness

God speaks to me: my child, look around you. See the world you are in and its demands. Respond to it and live in it! Even those who are professionally dedicated to the exclusive pursuit of the virtues and the contemplative life have to concern themselves with the mundane tasks of daily life, and the ever-ongoing concerns for the earth they are charged to care for. Tasks like your daily livelihood and responsibilities like a concern for ecology and relief for the poor and suffering of the world must be attended to. Indeed, at times, these will so occupy you that you will fear you are not giving me enough attention.

Know that your spiritual strength can be restored by such loving responses to the needs of others. Even in the middle of the humble pursuits you are called to perform in your service, call upon me. Await and expect me to show myself. With open heart and mind receive my encouragement and support, which will never be lacking to you. I can make you forget your troubles and experience that my yoke is sweet and my burden light. In your busiest days, among your most distracting tasks, lift your mind and heart to me in a moment of love and all will be well. Everything will be well.

Keep in touch, even if only briefly, by fidelity to your daily prayers. Read and meditate on the scriptures. Give me only a few moments of your time and you will be amazed at my responses.

✦ 52

What Is It That You Really Deserve?

I speak to the Lord: Father, you love me in spite of the unloving things I have done. It is not your will that the creature you made should perish. I cannot deny the reality of my sins, of my unloving attitude toward you, toward others, and toward myself. When I look at the things I have done, at the omissions I am guilty of, I am covered with confusion. Surely I am the prodigal child who kneels at your feet to say: "Father, I am not worthy to be your child." I do not deserve comfort from you. What would I be like to someone who treated me as I have treated you? How heavily I count on the unconditional nature of your love. You do not console me because I deserve it, but because I need it.

I confess my sins to you because from my sorrow arises hope for your pardon. Your pardon is always offered to me. I know that you say, "I forgive you" before I sin, while I am sinning, and after I have sinned. Your pardon, as your love, is unconditional. You do not say "I will forgive you when . . . " or "I will forgive you provided that . . ." or "I will forgive you if. . . . " You simply say over and over again, "My child, I love you and I forgive you." However, for me to be able to hear and receive this pardon, I have to open myself by acknowledging my faults and asking for forgiveness.

Like the father of the prodigal son, you are always watching to see me return. You are waiting for me. It is your grace that calls me home when I am beside myself in a foreign land having wasted all of my inheritance. I confess my faults before you and rejoice to hear those words, "This, my child, was dead and has come back to life; was lost and is found." Thus I know that whatever is broken can be mended. Whatever is soiled can once again be washed clean.

✦ 53
We Need to Be with God in God's Creation and in Godself

God speaks to me: my child, if you really wish to be close to me, you must take the necessary means. There are times when you will know I am near you in the midst of your dutiful occupations. You will see and feel me in and with your loved ones. I will reveal myself in laughter, in companionship, and in the good things of my creation. I will also be present in crosses and sometimes I will be closest to you when I seem to be farthest away.

Try to realize also that there are times when you need to be with me alone. You must arrange for those times each day or, at the very least, several times a week. Yes, you love me when you love others and even yourself, but you must also love me in and for myself. I speak to you through other people and through the events, happy or sad, of your life, but often I will speak to you most intimately when you are alone with me and when you cannot run to distracting relationships or occupations. You need to hear me in silence and in leisure, in thoughtful reflections, *lectio divina,* and face-to-face confrontation.

It is in this sense that you must be detached from every created thing, even yourself. Detachment, even from good things, is real freedom. Without real freedom you cannot hear me or follow me without straying. You must especially be detached from yourself to live a spiritual life. No victory is greater than to triumph over oneself. When you do this, there is nothing left to hold you back from me. This is a true union of wills, the highest pinnacle of love.

Self-love that turns in upon itself as a decision goal for your activity will eventually destroy you. Superficially it seems to act for your enhancement, to fulfill your desires. In fact, it does the opposite. That is why it must be vigorously attacked and cut off at the roots. As hard as it will be, once accomplished, the destruction of self-love and the me-first attitude will leave you in peace and inward quiet. You must rise above yourself if you are to walk with me. Do not worry, I will help you but you must give the needed time and attention.

✦ 54

A Look at the Relationship between Nature and Grace

God speaks to me: my child, there are times when nature and grace work together. This should not present problems. However, there are other times, perhaps more frequently when they are opposed. I speak here of your fallen nature, those wounds carried by the entire human race, and which are found in human society as a whole as well as in every individual.

Sometimes the opposition between nature and grace is so subtle that they cannot be seen as different. By nature you desire what is good, especially myself. Thus there is always some good in what you strive for. This makes it easy for you to be deceived and to be taken in by a type of good that only has the appearance of good.

Your human nature is bent and crafty. It will betray you when not under the influence of my grace, seeking its own ends in place of me for whom it was created. My grace is open, honest, and seeks me directly. It does not seek to rationalize but speaks directly to your conscience or your better self. Grace prompts you to seek me directly and immediately. While your fallen nature is both to be obedient or to be overcome, my grace will accept discipline to live under my direction, which is the only way to personal freedom.

Grace honestly ascribes all honor and praise to me where it belongs. It will call upon you sometimes to accept injustice and dishonor for the name of Jesus. Your nature will cry out in protest. It is absorbed in worldly matters, looks toward material gain, and is easily aroused to anger when unsatisfied or criticized. Grace is not concerned by the loss of worldly goods because its joy is in heaven free from rust and decay.

Where nature is greedy, grace is generous. Grace truly believes from personal experience that giving is better than receiving. Nature leads you to believe that the lusts of the body are worthwhile and to be pursued. It can easily prompt you to forget the real values that will lead you to me. Once satisfied, however, you will be left with emptiness and shame. Grace will seek comfort in me alone, and leave you with peace and contentment even in the midst of struggle.

Your earthly nature will take pride in worldly values, possessions, and superficial admiration. It is eager to receive praise and admiration for its good deeds, and often does them simply for that end. It seeks the friendship of those who have power and wealth. It flatters them and basks in their favor. When things do not go its way, it grumbles. It will be vindictive and strive only for its own glorification.

When my grace seeks to be present in your life it will seek only those worldly goods that it needs to serve its neighbor and me. It will try to love its enemies. It will help and respect the poor. It will honor the rich only insofar as they show themselves to be truly my servants. It will endure poverty when it is necessary and refer all things to me.

Grace will teach you to control your self-love and overcome your fallen ways. It will seek my approbation over the superficial praises of men and women. Its one great desire is that my name be glorified. Grace is a special gift from me and sign of favor. It restores my lost image in men and women, calls them to love the things of heaven, and promises eternal salvation.

✦ 55
On the Power of God's Grace

I speak to God: yes, Lord, I am made in your image and likeness. It is your grace, your help, which works in me to restore that tarnished image that brings light to that shadowed likeness. If I am ever to be reunited to you, to turn from the idolatrous selfishness that makes me worship my own darkened nature, it will be only because of the grace you shower upon me through the merits of Jesus Christ. Without this I am lost. How strong, Lord, are the promptings of my flesh even when I know them to be misleading and destructive.

If there is one thing that I know, my God, it is that I need your grace and in abundance! I do not know precisely *what* original sin is, but I am certain *that* it is. It seems that, at times, my experience of my fallen nature is stronger than my experience of your grace and the victory that Christ has won for me. Left to myself, I am headed for destruction. I do sense some spark of light in my mind, which tells me of my inabilities, but of itself it cannot restore to me that which you recognized at the time of creation: that which you made was very good.

Lord, I must cry out to you with St. Paul, "The evil I would not, that I do. The good that I would do, that I do not." I know that you are good and the source of all goodness. I know that you are my salvation and the cause of all real happiness now and hereafter. Often I remind myself of this and yet I find myself time and time again wandering off to serve my sensual feelings against the dictates of my reasoning. The desire to do good is within me but often the strength is not there.

Lord, I do the only thing that is left for me. I give up! I throw myself at your mercy as a helpless child. It will never be my merits, my virtues, or my talents that will save me. What else can I do but fall down before you and let my feebleness draw from you grace and love? I will depend entirely upon you. I will act with your strength, hope on your promises, believe in your truth, and love with your very being. Your grace is enough for me. With it I can jump over any wall, run any race, carry any cross, win any battle.

Let your grace, Lord, be always before me and behind me. Let it be above me and below me, on my right hand and my left. Let it be within me and without me, my light, my truth, and my way.

✦ 56
We Must Listen to the Invitation of Christ, *"Come and Follow Me"*

God speaks to me: my child, you know from personal experience that you do not know the way. You are ignorant of the truth and you do not have of yourself any real life. Can you see how I am allowing your feebleness to lead you to me and realize that only I am your way, your truth, and your life?

I am your way. I offer you direction, a calling, a path that leads to my kingdom. It is not only through battling the forces of evil within you that you will come to me. You are also called to look toward the building of my kingdom in your world. You are called to labor in my vineyard using whatever talents I have given you and responding to whatever people and areas of need that my compassion in you directs. Your salvation is not an isolated thing.

I am your truth. I will never deceive you. You must constantly reach out in my direction to know that you have not given in to the wiles of the world, the flesh, and the devil. I am the truth that you must believe, as you continue to pray and to meditate on the scriptures and examine the lives of my holy ones of the past and the present.

✦ 57

To Err Is Human. It is Not an Occasion for Depression, but to Begin Again

God speaks to me: it pleases me when you are humble and patient with yourself and with your weaknesses. Do not be upset when everything does not go well with you. It is to your advantage to have people criticize you and even speak ill of you. You take such things too much to heart, as though they really mattered. Be concerned about what I think of you, because you know it is accurate. You also know I am understanding and compassionate.

You are full of good advice to others and know how to encourage them, but when it comes to yourself you do not know how to take that same advice. It does not take much to discourage you. Always remember that adversity strengthens, tension is a sign of life, and even the wildest accusations usually contain a grain of truth.

I am always ready to help you. So call on me rather than give in to the temptation to treat your accusers in the same manner they deal with you. Certainly you will feel the blow of unkind or false accusations. The degree to which you reel from these blows and the length of time you spend brooding over them will be a measure of your self-love. Let such events be an occasion of turning to me. Place the whole thing, people, and events, into my hands. Wait it out with patience and humility.

I lift up those who are bowed down. And you do, after all, tend to exaggerate the severity of your accusers' claims. Do you feel the same anxiety, distress, and anger or depression when a third party is the victim of the same kind of treatment? Don't worry when you find yourself in trouble or when you have to deal with the temptation to give as much as you get from others. You are only flesh and blood. I do not even expect an angelic response from you. Start over each day and you will be able to look back at a lifetime of new beginnings. This will please me greatly.

I speak to God: Lord, all's well that ends well. If I start over each day, then I will begin and end well. I know I have your interest and support. Your love as expressed in your promises will carry me through. Do not let me be so involved in my personal cares that I do not see you reaching out to me or even standing beside me when I need you most.

✦ 58
Many Devotions for Many Persons

God speaks to me: my child, appreciate the love I have for you and be grateful for the ways this is acted out in your life. Do not be concerned about others and my dealings with them except to be of help to them. If I seem to treat others better than you, know and accept that I have my reasons. Consider also that those very people may be envious of the treatment I mete out to you. Everybody has his or her own crosses. Some are more visible than others. Never be envious of others especially in their seeming success in serving me. Rejoice with them. After all is not this what you desire above all things—that my name be glorified in everything and everybody?

Beware of trying to magnify a particular devotion over others. There are many forms of devotions available in my church. This is not because one is better than another, but because there are many different kinds of people in the church who are attracted to me in different ways. Any devotion that causes my children to turn to me in faith, hope, and love, the service of others and care for the earth, is pleasing to me and should not be discouraged in favor of a "better devotion." Something is seriously wrong when any person or group of people present their particular spiritual attractions as superior to others.

Be cautious also, my child, of multiplying your devotions imprudently. Is it really virtuous to go around with your neck weighed down with every form of medal or pious object available? Likewise, how prudent is it to feel that your day is not complete unless you go through the entire gamut of lengthy prayers belonging to a dozen different devotions? Follow your attractions and let others follow theirs. Be pleased with the many choices my children have to help them in their spiritual path, and gently encourage them in a peaceful and moderate way.

✦ 59

We Hope and Trust Only in God

I speak to God: my Lord, it is only you that I can rely on in this life and the next. No comforts that I have received in an earthly manner can ever equal the consolations that you have given me. No earthly advice has ever been so effective as your counsels. When I seek to be aware of your presence with me, things go well even when they are difficult or painful. When you abide in me, hold my hand, or lead me on my path, I am richer than the wealthiest of men or women. When I consider the greatness of your promises and their true worthiness, what more could I ask for?

You know what my needs are. You recognize my weaknesses and send me whatever trials I need to become strong. You never err in your advice or refuse to show me the truth about myself. How confident I can be, how sure of the way when you are showing it to me. From you I have everything I need to live a successful life—one that will become eternal life. Everything that happens to me you allow only for my good even when it seems harsh or confusing. This, I believe, Lord, and offer you my thanks.

Lord, you are my only real hope and into your hands I place myself, all those whom I love and, indeed, all of your creation. There are things that all the riches of the world cannot influence. There are needs that the most influential people or the greatest number of friends cannot respond to. There is advice so peculiar to my personal needs that no one but you can understand.

If you are not with me, Lord, then nothing else can help, nothing matters. I cannot be happy apart from you. Without you my mind is confused, my heart is empty, and my world has no meaning. There is no home for me where you do not dwell, no friendship that is not inspired by your love, and no goal that falls short of you.

Nothing but you, Lord, can bring me peace and joy. All the goods of the earth are shallow and empty unless they can facilitate my approach to you. Continue to bless me, Lord, with the true wealth that never ceases to pour forth from your open hands. Cleanse my mind and purify my heart that nothing may be found in me that does not reflect your image. Be with me that I may be with you. No matter how well things may seem to be going, I am in exile and wandering in a vale of tears until I am home with you. Into your hands, O Lord, I commend my spirit.

BOOK FOUR

◆ ◆ ◆

An Encouragement to Become and to Live as the Body of Christ

The Lord Speaks to Me:
Do not work for the food that perishes,
but for the food that endures
for eternal life (Jn 6, 27).*

*Scriptural citations are from the *Oxford Annotated Bible.*

The Eucharist Foretold

The Lord speaks to me: Moses rose early in the morning, and built an altar at the foot of the mountain, and set up twelve pillars, corresponding to the twelve tribes of Israel. He sent young men of the people of Israel, who offered burnt offerings and sacrificed oxen as offerings of well-being to the Lord. Moses took half of the blood and put it in basins, and half of the blood he dashed against the altar. Then he took the book of the covenant, and read it in the hearing of the people, and they said, "What the Lord has spoken we will do and we will be obedient." Moses took the blood and dashed it on the people, and said, "See the blood of the covenant that the Lord has made with you in accordance with all these words" (Ex 24:4–8).

I speak to the Lord: Lord, even at the foot of Mt. Sinai at the very beginning of the events in the salvation history of your people, you tell us of the coming and the meaning of the body and blood of Christ, the Eucharist. The evening before Moses had this great sacrificial offering, he had told the people what God wanted of them. They replied, "All the words that the Lord has spoken we will do" (Ex 24:3). This is, as it were, a promise to respond to Jesus' command some twelve hundred years later. "Do this in memory of me." Now some two thousand years later we, the people of God, continue to respond.

Moses took the sacrificial blood, a symbol of the exclusive power of God over life, and returned half of it to God by dashing it on the altar, another symbol of God. The other half, the blood, symbol of God-given life, he sprinkled on the people. It became the blood that sealed the covenant of the people with God—the pledge by which they would obey God's commands and receive the call to union.

We recall, Lord, that along with the altar, a symbol of yourself, Moses also set up twelve pillars of stone, a symbol of the people of Israel. How easy it is to see here the foretelling of Jesus at the Last Supper along with the new Israel, the twelve apostles, offering them his blood, now the seal of a new covenant, one of love expressed in sacrifice. Already in this scene in the Book of Exodus we see the beginnings of an identification of the people with their God through a life-giving and a life-receiving sacrifice. O Lord, we join with them in their promise, "All the words that the Lord has spoken we will do."

◆ 2
The Beginnings of the Eucharist

The Lord speaks to me: then Moses called all the elders of Israel and said to them, "Go, select lambs for your families and slaughter the Passover lamb. Take a bunch of hysop, dip it in the blood that is in the basins, and touch the lintel and the two doorposts with the blood in the basin. None of you shall go outside the door of your house until morning. For the Lord will pass through to strike down the Egyptians; when he sees the blood on the lintel and on the two doorposts, the Lord will pass over that door and will not allow the destroyer to enter your houses to strike you down. You shall observe this rite as a perpetual ordinance for you and your children.... And the people bowed down and worshiped" (Ex 12:21–26).

I speak to God: the meaning, Lord, is here for me to see. Clearly, Jesus is the Passover lamb who was slain for us. By his blood we have been saved. The destroyer will not enter our houses nor will any abiding harm afflict your people. We have been saved by his blood. In each Eucharist we relive this great mystery and tell in word and action the story to our children in succeeding generations.

John the Baptist attested to this when he identified Jesus as the lamb of God. When Jesus died on the cross, it was at the time of the evening sacrifice in the nearby temple where the Passover was being commemorated. How often, Lord, should we remind ourselves that we have been sprinkled with the blood of the lamb? We have been redeemed by the death and rising of your Christ. He has won the victory for us.

Your work of salvation has been ongoing at various levels and degrees since it was first called for at the very origins of the human race. It became particularized with a special people, concretized with their deliverance from bondage in Egypt, furthered by their trials in the desert, and brought to a symbolic fruition by their entrance into a land flowing with milk and honey.

All of this, Lord, I recognize as a wonderful foretelling of our final and everlasting salvation through the death and resurrection of Jesus. The promises, the trials, and the decisive victory are lived out by all your children collectively and individually.

✦ 3
On the Body of Christ

God speaks to me: just as the body is one and has many members, and all the members of the body, though many, is one body, so it is with Christ. For in the one Spirit we were all baptized into one body—Jews or Greeks, slaves or free—and we were all made to drink of one Spirit. Indeed, the body does not consist of one member but of many. If the foot would say, "Because I am not a hand, I do not belong to the body," that would not make it any less a part of the body. And if the ear would say, "Because I am not an eye, I do not belong to the body," that would not make it any less a part of the body. If the whole body were an eye, where would the hearing be? If the whole body were hearing, where would the sense of smell be? But as it is, God arranged the members in the body, each one of them, as he chose. If all were a single member, where would the body be? . . . If one member suffers, all suffer together with it; if one member is honored, all rejoice together with it. Now you are the body of Christ and individually members of it (1 Cor 12:12–27).

I speak to God: at this time, Lord, you and I are speaking about the Eucharist, the body and blood of Christ. I do understand why you are reminding me through your inspired word about the body of Christ. In the wisdom of your revelation you wish me to be open to a marvelous truth. Even while the body of Christ is the Eucharist, it is the church, head and members. Yet I know that one does not come before the other, but the church and the Eucharist are wonderfully one so that neither has its real meaning without the other. Neither exists without the other and there is a mutual interdependence so united that to speak of the body of Christ and the people of God is to speak at once of the same mysterious, human and divine, sacramental reality.

I remember the ancient patristic teaching that the church was born out of the side of the crucified Savior. When water and blood flowed from his Sacred Heart at the supreme moment of his self-giving, there was present the church of Christ, the people of God, the body of Christ, head and members. The two, indeed, were one.

✦ 4

On the Body of Christ and Liturgical Prayer

Christ speaks to me: my child, there are many kinds and levels of prayer. I would have you know the special nature of liturgical prayer because it is the prayer of the body of Christ. It is the prayer of the entire church united together with me as its head as we effect, in the power of the Holy Spirit, creation's return to the Father. I offer this prayer to my Father and you offer it to me as my very own body, and through me to our eternal Father. I am always present in my church, but I am especially active as I exercise my priestly office in the liturgical celebrations. It follows from this that the liturgy, as my prayer and the prayer of my body the church, is a prayer that surpasses all others. The liturgy, the highest form of which is the eucharistic sacrifice of the Mass, is the fullness of the church being what it truly is and at the same time being the source from which all its power and efficacy flows.

I speak to Christ: Lord, help me to make my prayer genuine. I must realize that even liturgical prayer must be interior as well as exterior. The shared interior attitudes of your people united with you are the chief elements that make liturgical prayer sincere and genuine. It must not be mere words and actions no matter how splendidly performed.

Herein lies the value of private, devotional prayer. It leads to and flows from efficacious liturgical worship. Not only do I relate to you, Lord, through and with the other members of your body, but also I have a special, emotional, and affective relationship that is uniquely personal, necessary for my salvation and useful for the entire body of the church.

✦ 5

The Eucharist Is the Life of the Church

Christ speaks to me: my child, my Eucharist is the ever-flowing fountain of life, grace, and blessings, which I pour into the functioning of the living church. Everything in the church, the sacraments, the various ministries, the corporal and spiritual works of mercy, lead to it and flow from it. The Eucharist is the cause of the unity of the people of God and the source of the divine life that holds the church in being.

✦ 6

The Real Presence of Christ in the Prayer of the Church

Jesus speaks to me: my child, I promised to be with you always. I am present to you and to my church in many ways. Indeed, if the church is the body of Christ, it is itself my presence. You are accustomed to speak of my real presence in the Eucharist, but you must extend my presence in many ways. Wherever I am, I am really present. I cannot be present in any unreal way. Nor can I be present in any way that does not share in the fullness of who I am in the reality of my risen body and all that that means.

I speak to Jesus: yes, Lord, I am grateful for the ways you are present in our world. As the Word of God you hold all things in being by your presence. You reflect God's image in the beauties of creation, in the orderly laws of nature, and in the relationships of love found in the human family.

Jesus speaks to me: yes, my child, you are right to see me in all these ways. I am also present in the poor and suffering of the world and in those who would alleviate their misery. Let me speak to you also of my presence, my real presence in the liturgical celebrations of the church. In these ways I would give meaning to my presence in my suffering children and to their service, for whatever you do to the least of my brothers and sisters you do to me.

I am present in the liturgical celebration of the Mass, in the person of the celebrant who acts in my name. Also, when someone administers the sacraments, I am present in that ministry. I am present in the Eucharist. I am present in my word, which is read in the liturgy, and I am present wherever two or three gather together in my name.

Please keep in mind, my child, that when I say I am present, I mean that I am really present in each of these five ways in the liturgy. What is the difference then in my "real presence"? The difference is the manner or the modality of my presence. When the priest celebrates Mass, I am present as offering my sacrifice. When someone, duly authorized, administers the sacraments, I am present in the modality of dispensing my grace. When the scriptures are read, I am present in the manner of teaching the inspired word. When two or three are gathered in my name, I am present in the modality of my church. In the Eucharist I am present in the manner of feeding the faithful with my body and blood. The modalities or the ways of being present differ but the presence is the same. It is really I, the risen Christ, body and blood, soul and divinity, who is present and encountered in action and power.

As you can see, my child, my presence in the Eucharist is special but is not the only way I am present to the church. It is indeed a unique presence. All of my other ways of being present are through the activity of the church in administering grace and holy teaching. This is true also of the eucharistic sacrifice, but there is an objective abiding element in the Eucharist by which I am present in a permanent way as long as the species of bread and wine endures.

For many centuries my eucharistic presence, reserved in the tabernacles, was kept only for distribution to the sick and some others who could not assist at the liturgy. Most often these tabernacles were simply special places reserved in the homes of priests. Then they were placed in the churches for availability to all the faithful who wished to worship me in my eucharistic real presence. Such devotion was enhanced in the thirteenth century by great saints like St. Francis and St. Thomas Aquinas. The festival of Corpus Christi, known more completely now as the Feast of the Body and Blood of Christ, was established to honor and facilitate popular devotion to the Eucharist.

✦ 7

The Eucharist as Presence and the Eucharist as Presence-Given-as-Food-and-Drink

I speak to the Lord: Lord, devotion to your eucharistic presence reserved in our tabernacles has been a powerful element in the church for at least the last eight hundred years. In response to popular devotion, tabernacles since the thirteenth century took a central place in most of our churches and were relocated to the high altars. In recent years the church has mandated that they be taken from that central position and located in another less obvious place in the churches. For many of us this is difficult to understand.

The Lord speaks to me: my child, devotion to my presence in the Eucharist is a laudable and almost inevitable result of the reverend reflection of the faithful. However, in some ways, the response to my real presence led to a reverence that was overwhelming. The members of the body of Christ held the sacramental body of Christ in such awe and respect that they lost a significant element of its true meaning. The modality or manner of my presence in the Blessed Sacrament is not primarily the presence of the body and blood to-be-worshiped. It is the presence of the body and blood to-be-received, to-be-eaten, and thus to be the supernatural nourishment of the body of Christ, which is the church.

The awesome respect for my eucharistic presence caused the faithful to be afraid to receive my body and blood. They did not consider themselves worthy to be sharers in my supper, so awestruck were they by my real presence. They would worship me from afar in the tabernacle but were afraid to seek union with me by following my command to "take and eat." In an effort to counteract this unhappy attitude, the church actually made legislation, still in force, that the faithful had to receive the Eucharist at least once a year during Easter season.

In more recent times only did the reception of the Eucharist revert to the practice of the early church where all who were worthy to be present at the liturgy and who qualified spiritually would receive the Eucharist. It was to avoid a return to the sad neglect of receiving my body and blood that prompted the church to remove the tabernacles from the high altars and place them in a place especially reserved in the churches. The church is saying by this: "Yes, the Eucharist is to be adored and this will be provided for. However, the most important thing to remember is that the Eucharist is to be received and the real presence of the body and blood of Christ in the life and activity of the church is to be appreciated and stressed." The body and blood of Christ are given for us. It is an activity that calls for an active reception and a lived-out response to the great commandment of love. The central place in the churches is reserved for the altar, itself a symbol of my presence and around which the people of God are to gather to celebrate my supper, my giving of myself to them in the context of my death and resurrection. It is a place for the body of Christ to be nourished by the body of Christ and to be reaffirmed in the oneness of their union in me.

◆ 8

A Sacrifice and a Communion

Jesus speaks to me: sacrifice or offering has been an important element in the worship of God since the beginnings of the human race. The shedding of blood, often an essential element of sacrifice, was an acknowledgment and a returning to God of the great gift of life. Very often a meal was associated with this sacrifice. This symbolized God's sharing or returning the gift of life to those who offered it. Thus there was accomplished a communion with God and a communion among the worshipers.

You can see, my child, how the covenants with Noah (Gn 8:20), with Abraham (Gn 15:9), and with Moses (Ex 12:21), called for a meal, which was a food sacrifice. They were the seals for mutual agreements between God and his people. The Passover meal was especially significant. The agreement from God's past was to liberate

God's people, to free them from bondage. An important part of this memorial meal was the command to repeat it. "This day shall be a day of remembrance for you. You shall celebrate it as a festival to the Lord; throughout your generations you shall observe it as a perpetual ordinance" (Ex 12:14).

✦ 9

The New Sacrifice and the New Covenant

Jesus speaks to me: while they were eating, Jesus took a loaf of bread, and after blessing it he broke it, gave it to the disciples, and said, "Take, eat; this is my body." Then he took a cup, and after giving thanks he gave it to them, saying, "Drink from it, all of you; for this is my blood of the covenant, which is poured out for many for the forgiveness of sins."

I speak to the Lord: thank you, Jesus, for sharing again with me these incredible words and this awesome event. Let me consider some of the things you are sharing with me. I can see now that these are not just words instituting the Eucharist. There is an activity involved here, which you present as a command. You do not say simply, "This is my body." What you say is, "Take and eat, this is my body." Also you say something similar with the cup. You do not say, "This is my blood." You say, "Drink from it, all of you, for this is my blood of the covenant."

Precisely what is it, Lord, that we are to do in memory of you when we reenact this supper? We are to eat and drink the body and blood of Christ as the seal of a new and perpetual covenanted agreement with God. God is to be our God, we are to be God's people. God will be one with us, uniting us to each other, and we will live the real presence and our union with each other by restoring God's image and likeness in ourselves and our society. This is the new covenant. It will be carried out by loving. God will love us and we will love God and, for God's sake, one another.

It is clear to us, Lord Jesus, from the reading of the scriptures and the teaching of the church, that the language you use here is the language of sacrifice. It will be the sacrifice of yourself, of your body and blood, which will seal this covenant. No longer the blood of animals, but the blood of the lamb of God.

We also are made, by this sharing in your body and blood, partakers of this sacrifice. We are lifted up on the cross with you. We are called to die with you and to rise with you. Your sufferings become ours and we make our sufferings yours. Our crosses become one. Meaning and significance is given to our trials, our sorrows, even our weaknesses. The victory that you will win over sin and death becomes our victory.

✦ 10

One Eucharist, One Covenant, One Sacrifice

The Lord speaks to me: nor did Jesus offer himself again and again, as the high priest enters the holy place year after year with blood that is not his own; for then he would have to suffer again and again since the foundation of the world. But as it is, he has appeared once for all at the end of the age to remove sin by the sacrifice of himself (Heb 9:25–26).

I speak to the Lord: how wonderful it is, my Lord, that we have such a sacrifice. It is not that you die and rise again every time the Eucharist is offered but that your one, complete, and eternal sacrifice is made present to us in every Mass. You have given your supper an ecclesial dimension so that it may be memorialized everywhere and at every time in the church. The same body of Christ, always with new members, is eating and drinking your flesh and blood, sealing the new covenant with your blood, and living out in their daily lives your commandment of love. It is by doing this in memory of you that we perpetuate the reality of your death and resurrection until you come in glory.

✦ 11

The Eucharist as a Pledge of Eternal Life

The Lord speaks to me: I am the bread of life. Whoever comes to me, will never be hungry, and whoever believes in me, will never be thirsty

... this is the will of my Father that all who see the Son and believe in him, may have eternal life; and I will raise them up on the last day. ... Very truly I tell you whoever believes has eternal life. I am the bread of life ... I am the living bread that comes down from heaven. Whoever eats of this bread will live forever; and the bread that I will give for the life of the world, is my flesh ... unless you eat the flesh of the Son of man and drink his blood, you have no life in you. Those who eat my flesh and drink my blood have eternal life, and I will raise them up on the last day; for my flesh is true food and my blood is true drink. Those who eat my flesh and drink my blood abide in me and I in them. Just as the living Father sent me and I live because of the Father, so whoever eats me will live because of me. This is the bread that came down from heaven, not like that which your ancestors ate, and they died. But the one who eats this bread will live forever (Jn 6:35f.).

I speak to the Lord: my Jesus, you have the words of eternal life.

✦ 12
On Full Sharing in the Liturgy

The Lord speaks to me: my child, it is important that each one of my people who is present at the eucharistic sacrifice exercises his or her full role. The priest acts in my person and offers the sacrifice in the name of all the people of God. The people who are themselves the body of Christ and a royal priesthood by reason of their baptism join in the offering. They offer the sacred victim and themselves together with him, not only by way of the hands of the priest, but also with him.

The celebration of Mass is the action of the assembled people of God and their head who is Christ. It is very significant that the liturgical celebration allow the fullest participation possible for all who are present and who bring to it their inner dispositions of faith, hope, and charity. They will thus be enabled by God's grace to carry out into their diverse callings the fullest meaning of the new covenant that they have memorialized. This is what is meant by living the Mass.

✦ 13

The Eucharist as Sacrament and Sign

The Lord speaks to me: my child, know that all of the sacraments are effective signs that cause the graces they symbolize. They proceed directly or indirectly from my hands and I am present when they are administered. This is true, in a very special way of the Eucharist.

I speak to the Lord: yes, Lord, I understand that the symbol of nourishment is crucial to an understanding of your Eucharist. You give yourself to us under the form of the commonest of foods served even on the tables of the poor, bread and wine. You command us, at every eucharistic celebration, to eat and drink because you are the bread of life. Your flesh is food, indeed, and your blood is drink indeed. The nourishment that the Eucharist symbolizes, it also brings about in us. By your presence our wounds are healed, our sins are forgiven, and our spiritual growth is assured.

✦ 14

On a Lack of Fervor in Participating in the Liturgy and Receiving Holy Communion

I speak to the Lord: I accept, Lord, the truly awesome teachings you give us about the Eucharist as sacrifice and sacrament. Because it is your greatest gift to us, the gift of yourself. I am dismayed at my frequent inability to give myself with proper devotion and attention. What can I do, Lord, to open myself to your presence, your nourishment, and your graces?

The Lord speaks to me: my child, you are right to recognize this deficiency in yourself. What you must do is continually ask for the grace of devotion. The very fact of your asking is an awareness of your need and a positive step forward in fulfilling it. Wait for my response to your prayer with patience and confidence. I desire the same thing for you as you seek for yourself. Between the two of us, we will bring it about.

Be humble in your searching, my child. Humility is simply facing the truth about yourself and your needs. Nothing better serves the need to open your mind and heart. Humility is incompatible with complacency.

Do not allow yourself to be unduly depressed about your lack of devotion. At times your devotion is much greater than you realize. The simple fact of perseverance over long periods without palpable zeal is itself a powerful show of real devotion. It shows that you are seeking me rather than my gifts. Often I will give you in a brief moment so intense a devotion that you do not even realize it at the time. Only on looking back at what may seem a long period of dryness will you recognize the extraordinary graces I have given you.

Be conscious, my child, of barriers that you may place in the way of my grace. Subtle habits bordering on sinfulness, a willful neglect of personal prayer, spiritual reading, or meditation will hinder your appreciation of the great mysteries you are called to enter in the liturgy. The power of the world, in a negative sense, is very much with you. You are besieged every day, almost every hour, with appeals to values that are not mine. Ambition, selfishness, more and more material possessions are all a part of your environment. You need, at regular intervals, to go apart, to a desert place. By that I mean a place or retreat that is, to some extent, free of the clamorous cries to worldly values. Take stock of yourself. Examine your conscience. This will speedily open the way for grace and a deeper devotion. What you bring to the liturgy, even if it is only an awareness of your needs and weaknesses, will enhance what you receive from it. Suppose, at a given time, the only thing you receive is an intense awareness of your need for me. Is this not of itself a great grace? When this happens surrender yourself to me. Throw yourself before me and I will give you myself.

Remember, my child, when you receive the Eucharist, I do give myself to you whether you feel it or not. Do not be concerned with your own comfort. This is a chance for you to love unconditionally and to seek above all things my honor and glory. For those who love me, all things work together for good.

✦ 15

On the Word and the Eucharist

Jesus speaks to me: now on that same day two of them were going to a village called Emmaus, about seven miles from Jerusalem, and talking with each other about all these things that happened. While they were talking and discussing, Jesus himself came near but their eyes were kept from recognizing him (Lk 24:13f.).

I speak to Jesus: these two disciples, Lord, had left Jerusalem, which was the city where you would reveal yourself to the church. They left without faith in your resurrection and were actually involved in a somewhat futile discussion of the events that had happened. The first step in their conversion to faith had to be taken by you. Even though you were not recognized, you presented yourself to them. All grace comes from you, Lord. We cannot recognize you until you reveal yourself to us.

The Lord speaks to me: and he said to them, "What are you discussing with each other while you walk along?" They stood still, looking sad. Then one of them, whose name was Cleopas, answered him, "Are you the only stranger in Jerusalem who does not know the things that have taken place there in these days?" He asked them: "What things." They replied, "The things about Jesus of Nazareth, who was a prophet mighty in deed and word before God and all the people, and how our chief priests and leaders handed him over to be condemned to death and crucified him. But we had hoped that he was the one to redeem Israel."

I speak to the Lord: I know, Lord, that here you are giving us a paradigm of the early church after your resurrection. They were saddened by your absence. Of themselves they were able to do nothing about how things were except perhaps in a mournful way to talk about them. It was your presence in, indeed, your eucharistic presence that brought them hope and faith. We have here in this account of the disciples on the road to Emmaus a somewhat literal description of the form the liturgy took on very early in the Church. There was first, as it is today, the liturgy of the word, an exposition of the meaning of the events of your death and resurrection. But the events themselves did not bring proof. They did not arouse the faith and hope that the church needed to see itself as being the body of the risen Christ. Only you could do this by your presence to the church in your word and in power. This you did.

The Lord speaks to me: "Yes," the disciples said, "and besides all this, it is now the third day since these things took place. Moreover some women of our group astounded us. They were at the tomb early this morning and when they did not find his body there, they came back and told us that they had indeed seen a vision of angels who said that he was alive. Some of those who were with us went to the tomb and found it just as the women had said; but they did not see him."

I speak to the Lord: it seems, Lord, that the empty tomb and the vision of angels reported by the women were not sufficient to bring faith in the resurrection to the disciples. They are symbolic of your early church. The only one who could really give faith to your people was yourself. You do this through your presence in the assembly gathered together to worship. First they listen and receive your word through the reading of the scriptures and the homily. This is what we see happened to the two disciples.

The Lord speaks to me: "oh, how foolish you are, and how slow of heart to believe all that the prophets have declared! Was it not necessary that the Messiah should suffer these things and then enter into his glory?" Then beginning with Moses and all the prophets, he interpreted to them all the things about himself in the scriptures.

I speak to the Lord: Lord, we have our own ideas, inspired by our worldly viewpoints about how things should have happened if we are to accept them as coming from God. You show us how wrong we are. You yourself are the source of faith and hope and love. We must listen to you. We depend on your explanation and your exposition of the meaning of salvation history. As often as the faithful gather to worship and to remember the events of revelation, you present yourself to them, often unrecognized, to confirm their faith and allay their fears.

The Lord speaks to me: as they came near the village to which they were going, he walked ahead as if he were going on. But they urged him strongly, saying, "Stay with us, because it is almost evening and the day is now nearly over." So he went in to stay with them.

I speak to the Lord: how beautiful, Lord, is this account. How powerful the prayer of the disciples even though they were ignorant of its full meaning. Still, they were offering shelter and nourishment to a stranger, one of the least of the brethren. How magnificent was your response to be. I must realize that this is not an event of the past but a daily occurrence in your church. Stay with us, Lord.

The Lord speaks to me: so he went in to stay with them. When he was at the table with them, he took bread, blessed and broke it, and gave it to them. Then their eyes were opened, and they recognized him and he vanished from their sight.

I speak to the Lord: this was Easter Sunday, Lord and you were the first to observe your own wish to "do this in memory of me." You celebrated the first Mass after the Last Supper and the resurrection. This was, indeed, your eucharistic presence acting and confirming the faith of your church. Now the disciples believed in your resurrection, not because of the empty tomb or even the vision of angels, but because you brought it to them yourself. I am reminded of your encounter with the woman at the well. She brought you to the people of her city by saying, "See, he has told me everything about myself," but after you stayed with them for several days, they said, "We believe now not because of what you said, but because we have experienced him ourselves."

This is what you do for us, Lord, even today in the eucharistic liturgy. Our eyes are opened and we recognize you in your word and in the breaking of the bread. Continue, Lord, to let our hearts burn within us as you open the scriptures and break the eucharistic bread for us.

The Lord speaks to me: that same hour they got up and returned to Jerusalem; and they found the eleven and their companions together. They were saying "the Lord has appeared to Simon!" Then they told what had happened on the road, and how he had been made known to them in the breaking of the bread.

I speak to the Lord: how often, Lord, have you blessed me with your presence, your wisdom and your body and blood in the breaking of the bread—in the eucharistic celebration. Give me the same eager desire you gave to the two disciples to share my faith so that hearts may burn at the good news of your risen presence among us today.

✦ 16
Which Deals with Prayer

I speak to God: Lord, I express my personal relationship with you by my prayer. Through the exchange of dialogue, which I understand as prayer, you exchange with me also the desires of your heart and the reality of your personal love. Teach me, Lord, what you will.

The Lord speaks to me: my child, look at the life of my Son, Jesus Christ, and see the priority he gave to the personal expression of his relationship with me. You can be sure that every time he did this I was responding in the very depths of his heart. The gospels show a consistent pattern of prayer in the public life of Jesus. He always began with prayer, then he took the fruits of prayer into the activity of his ministry. Then he would retire to be nourished again with and through me. Always before the important decisions and commitments of his ministry, he prayed. We see this especially before his passion and even on the cross. His prayer was quiet and peaceful when that is where he was. At other times it was emotional and even fearful. On the cross he was demanding and even on the border of despair. But always he prayed. Do you think, given his example and his need, that you need prayer any less than he did?

I speak to Jesus: dear Lord, I join with the plea of your disciples. Teach me how to pray. Bring me into the sacred, intimate, personal relationship that you have with the Father.

Jesus speaks to me: my child, I am pleased to share with you and encourage you in the ways of prayer. Always, you should watch and pray. Always you should pray and never lose heart. You need prayer in all the ways and levels that involves. It may sound strange at first but think of it. God does not need prayer, you do. God knows your needs, he knows your desire to praise and thank God, and knows your need to approach God in sorrow and repentance, But it is you who need to express these sentiments to God from your heart in sincerity and truth. You need to express your dependence on God's mercy; you need to know that God's grace is available to you by asking for it in prayer. Praying is a lifting your hands to the Father and experiencing his response as the father takes your uplifted hands and says, "Here I am. I give you myself. Whatever it is that you go through from joy to sorrow, I am with you." This, my child, is the bottom line. This is the ultimate answer to all your prayer. I am with you.

✦ 17
The Lord's Prayer

Jesus speaks to me: when you pray say, our Father who art in heaven. Hallowed be thy name. Thy kingdom come. Thy will be done on earth as it is in heaven. Give us this day our daily bread and forgive us our trespasses as we forgive those who trespass against us. Lead us not into temptation but deliver us from evil. Amen.

I speak to Jesus: yes, Lord, you have given us your own prayer. Because we are individually and collectively the body of Christ, we are privileged to say this prayer with you. This, above all, is what makes this prayer effective.

Jesus speaks to me: yes, my child, that is well said, but it is important for you to realize that I did not give this prayer as a series of words to be memorized. I really did answer the request to be taught how to pray that my disciples asked. This prayer contains the dispositions that your prayer, of any kind, must have if it is to be really my prayer. If your prayer follows these dispositions, it will be effective prayer. It will open doors, move mountains. It will be prayer asked truly in my name, which the Father will never refuse.

This is how you should pray. Always pray to your Father and mine. He loves us and we can turn to the Father with confidence. Our confidence comes from knowing that the Father is heavenly. The Father knows all and can do everything. We desire first the giver of the gifts even more than the gifts themselves. So our first desire is that our prayer and all that we wish be done for the glory of his name. Then we ask that the fullness of his kingdom be brought about. This will be the perfect accomplishment of his will. Anything we ask will conform to this priority if it is to be in my name. Then we seek from the Father the basic necessities of life. We do not ask for power, wealth, unnecessary comforts, or undue favors denied to others. We show the oneness of the body of Christ by conditioning our forgiveness from the Father on our willingness to forgive others. All men and women are brothers and sisters, and we will pray for each often. Finally, we ask of the Father the gift of final perseverance and the hope that will bring us home to the Father in glory.

Of related interest from Continuum

THOMAS KEATING

OPEN MIND, OPEN HEART

Written by an acknowledged modern spiritual master, the book moves beyond "discursive meditation and particular acts to the intuitive level of contemplation." Keating gives an overview of the history of contemplative prayer in the Christian tradition, and step-by-step guidance in the method of centering prayer.

158 pages

THOMAS KEATING

THE MYSTERY OF CHRIST
The Liturgy as Christian Experience

A reflection on the contemplative dimension of Christian worship. Focusing on the liturgical year, Abbot Keating shares his theological and mystical perspective on the major feasts of the annual cycle.

160 pages

THOMAS KEATING

INVITATION TO LOVE
The Way of Christian Contemplation

In this final volume of his trilogy, Abbot Keating offers a road map, as it were, for a journey that begins when centering prayer is seriously undertaken.

160 pages

THOMAS KEATING

CRISIS OF FAITH, CRISIS OF LOVE

Revised and Expanded Edition

"Under the influence of Christian mystics such as St. John of the Cross, Keating weaves a narrative account of spiritual development that will be of . . . interest to spiritual directors and seekers." —*Booklist*

140 pages

WILLIAM A. MENINGER

THE LOVING SEARCH FOR GOD

Contemplative Prayer and The Cloud of Unknowing

"Using the 14th-century spiritual classic *The Cloud of Unknowing* as both a jumping-off place and a sustained point of reference, Meninger, a Trappist monk and retreat master, does a powerful job of explaining contemplative prayer and making it approachable for any seeker. In a nurturing, practical and easy-to-understand manner, and with an obvious affection for his subject, Meninger deals with the yearning search for God through prayer and with the distractions that can impede it—unforgiveness and unforgivenness, will, distortions of imagination, memory, and intellect. The result, filled with humor and built by means of good, solid language that flows beautifully, is an excellent guide for anyone interested in deepening his or her Christian prayer life." —*Publishers Weekly*

120 pages

WILLIAM A. MENINGER
THE PROCESS OF FORGIVENESS

In this book, Father Meninger explores the complex, but most necessary facet of spiritual life: forgiveness. He shows how we can learn to make this the most simple, yet most difficult part of our spiritual practice.

112 pages

WILLIAM A. MENINGER
THE TEMPLE OF THE LORD
And Other Stories

Composed in the form of three stories which form a triptych illustrating the spiritual life, the book examines three important facets of Christian understanding: "The Temple of the Lord," "Wisdom Built a House," and "The Messiah God."

96 pages

JOHN R. AURELIO
RETURNINGS
Life-after-Death Experiences: A Christian View

"Easy to read and full of practical insight."
—*Booklist*

"So, very good! What a strength and consolation this will be for many people!" —Richard Rohr

120 pages

M. BASIL PENNINGTON

ON RETREAT WITH THOMAS MERTON

Fellow Cistercian monk and intimate friend of Merton, M. Basil Pennington wrote this book at Gethsemani Abbey where he lived in the hermitage where Merton spent his last five years. He offers an intimate glimpse of Merton's day-to-day living. With original photographs by Thomas Merton.

120 pages

M. BASIL PENNINGTON

THOMAS MERTON, BROTHER MONK

The Quest for True Freedom

"This is the Merton I knew—the seeker of God, the spiritual master. Each of the previous biographies has made its own unique contribution, but none has so explored the man's life. . . . a totally engaging and thoughtful work."

—James Finley

226 pages

LEONARD J. BOWMAN

A RETREAT WITH ST. BONAVENTURE

Bowman explicates the life of the Franciscan Bonaventure (1217–1274) for modern-day applications of his teachings.

204 pages